Jesus among the Gentiles

The Northern ministry of Jesus

J. Ben Pickering

Media & Publishing

Published in Melbourne, Australia
By Zenan Media and Publishing. 2013

**Zenan Media & Publishing
P.O. Box 3143
Ivanhoe North
Victoria. 3079**

© J. Ben Pickering 2014

By This Author:
- From Hate To Hope – The Vision of Obadiah
- Twelve Stones – The Breastplate
- The Shekhinah Glory
- I Think I've Burnt My Bushel!
- The Little Book of Talking With God
- Talking With God
- Jesus among the Gentiles

ISBN

978-0-9578006-8-7

This book

is dedicated to

my Brothers and Sisters

A Miracle Today

Are the days of miracles over?
I watch a bee upon the clover.
Jesus turned the water into wine
The sun is up the day is fine
Little miracles happen each day
It's up to us to think and pray

Has a miracle happened to you?
Can you see them in things you do?
You had an opportunity to serve
with enthusiasm and with verve.
Little miracles happen each day
So give thanks to God and say.

Thank you Lord for sending a friend
who will be with me to the end.
He tells me when I'm going wrong
and he'll correct my ways ere long.
Little miracles happen today
that turn me back into God's way.

Audrey Christophersen

Jesus among the Gentiles

The Northern ministry of Jesus

Contents...

Foreword	8
Introduction	10
A Saviour for the Nations	13
A Clean Heart	18
A Woman Asks	31
A Man Speaks	46
A Multitude Feed	71
A Lonely Loaf	97
A Brave New World	105

Foreword

By Peter P Osborn

Have you ever wondered who Jesus really is? I mean really deliberated upon who he was as a person who lived and talked and ate whilst walking around the region of Galilee of the Gentiles. What was Jesus really like, what kind of a person was he?

Jesus was a 'Jew', living in first-century Israel, living a first-century Jewish culture and lifestyle. We thoroughly recommend that you read JB's book, 'Jesus among the Gentiles', it becomes more real that this is the land where Jesus lived, died and rose from the dead and it is this land and people to which he will return. Read this book and it will help serve our purpose in life, which is to discover the historic Jesus and accept him as Messiah.

Having been privileged to visit Eretz Israel eight times, it was surprising to read a book that captures the very essence of the land of Israel. He describes the geography of Israel which is very diverse, with desert conditions in the south and snow-capped mountains in the north.

Jesus' encounters with Gentiles take place predominantly in the northern region which contains the Mount Carmel mountain range, which is followed inland by the fertile Jezreel Valley, and then the hilly Galilee region. The Sea of Galilee is located beyond this, and is bordered to the east by the Golan Heights and Mount Hermon.

This book, 'Jesus among the Gentiles' has captured the spirit of everyday life in the Galilean countryside and challenges us to imagine the very expressions of our Lord's face even as he outmanoeuvres the nonsense of the Pharisees.

JB has succeeded to enlighten us on the account of the feeding of the thousands – the expression 'bread of life' takes on a new meaning. There are beautiful parallels between the two accounts of feeding, so make a note of their locations and where the miracles were really taking place!

In John 10:16 Jesus says: *And I have other sheep that are not of this fold. I must bring them also, and they will listen to my voice. So there will be one flock, one shepherd.*

The common belief, as I understand it, is that this refers to the division between Jews and Gentiles. But when Jesus first sends out his disciples he specifically tells them not to preach to Gentiles.

Matthew 10:5-6: *These twelve Jesus sent out, instructing them, "Go nowhere among the Gentiles and enter no town of the Samaritans, but go rather to the lost sheep of the house of Israel."*

So what?

From the passages just cited and the fact that Jesus spent most of his time teaching Jews, it's not a stretch to say that Jesus saw his mission as limited to Israel. But JB reminds us that Jesus *did* go into the region of the Decapolis, which began as Greek colonies and at that time were heavily influenced by Rome. Jesus also visited Tyre and Sidon, which were ancient pagan cities. The Gospel of Mark emphasizes that he was there to get a break and that he only helped the Gentile woman while he was there because of her faith.

Jesus decided to take the disciples somewhere that is amazing, it would have been like taking the youth group to Las Vegas. In fact, Jesus takes the disciples to Caesarea Philippi for a special education. This is actually as far north that Jesus ever travelled in his ministry, so he went there to specifically teach his disciples something and he asked them, "Who do people say the Son of Man is?" We can see why Peter's confession was so striking in his answer - "You are the Messiah, the Son of the living God."

Be careful as you read this book that you do not experience sea sickness as you travel from one side of the Sea of Galilee to the other side and the region of the Decapolis. One thing is for sure, JB makes you wonder what it was really like to be in the company of our Lord and Teacher and you begin to imagine just how long it would have taken him to walk from place to place.

JB delves into the background of stories that we might be all too familiar with and then he pops up questions to help us see for ourselves many fascinating analogies - for example, in the lives of a Hebrew girl (the daughter of Jairus, a synagogue leader) and a Gentile girl (a Syrophoenician) who were probably about the same age. Don't miss these beautiful cameos of Jesus showing us his humanity and his compassion as he changed and empowered Jewish and Gentile lives forever!

The challenge we are left with is this, do we want to be touched by the Master? Salvation is all about the power of God but that means working this out up close and personal, being transformed this side of the Kingdom - and in JB's terminology, taking on this process and being 'totally blown away'.

Introduction

This was an enjoyable project to work on. I've recently been blessed with more time to spend on study and writing and it has been a real joy to be able to focus on what was really a small moment in time in the Gospel records. This study made sense as it progressed and the lessons were profound. In a way they are timeless too. They still speak at some volume even in today's very different world.

How Jesus touched people, reached out to them as we'll consider here – makes it evident that he really was very good at his job. I often think it must be a great privilege to be the Son of God – but what a huge responsibility it is also. Many of us have likewise been called to be sons and daughters of the Living God, which also comes with privileges and responsibilities, in this we have been immeasurably blessed to have the example of the Lord Jesus Christ.

If you were to write a Gospel instead of Matthew, Mark, Luke or John – what would you have written about? What part of the life and ministry of Jesus would you have concentrated on? There's nothing wrong with what we have with the Gospels but these writers were *affected* by what they saw and heard and were changed in their own lives by their experiences with the Son of God.

So the question is, what *affects* you? It could be many things or just a few. Perhaps there are times when you feel more strongly influenced by something that Jesus did. It was Jesus who taught us through the Gospels to address God as 'Our Father'.

He wanted us to have that sort of relationship with God (and God does too!) but the fact is we don't have that relationship, or cannot have that relationship until we first have a relationship with Jesus Christ because he is our Mediator.

In an endeavour to achieve this we have woven into the narrative of this book a few questions that you will be challenged to answer for yourself as you read. Most are subtle and you'll find yourself asking, 'Wow, what would I have done or said?'

I hope this study answers a few questions you may have had on this part of Jesus' life. Hopefully you'll find it enjoyable and take the questions further, applying them to other studies in which you challenge yourself. This is a relatively short book, it could have been longer or taken in more of the ministry of Jesus – but the point of this study was to take just one interesting section and make it come alive, demonstrating what anyone can find as they look into things of spiritual substance.

So, let's strap on our sandals and take a walk with Jesus!

God bless,

JBP

A SAVIOUR FOR THE NATIONS

Jesus. The mention of the name moves people. This name above any other stirs the imagination or an emotional response from the greater part of civilization.

For some that response is joy, for others it is wonder and for some it may be guilt or even breath-taking respect. If asked in a formal survey to articulate the first word that came to mind when they heard the name of Jesus, I think the majority would answer, 'Christianity'.

As general as that may be, for those who read and study the life and times of Jesus, there is a different word: Humanity. It is impossible to study his ministry, to read the greatest story ever recorded – and to not be touched by the sheer humanity of the man and the desperate humanity of those he taught, fed, healed, touched, walked with, ate with - and for whom he ultimately died and rose to life again.

He stood as an example for us in his life and represented us and our nature in his death but his life was all the more poignant because of the people he encountered. We relate with these people because they are just like us. Their response to situations in that time was just as we would respond today.

The work of Jesus didn't change humanity, not in a natural way yet at least; instead he sought to high-light through his own humanity a way of working *through* the difficulties and faults we all have, to draw us to his Father's eternal spirituality.

The frustrations of human nature are intertwined with the narrative of a Heavenly Father ready to reconcile and make His creation at one with Him again. The ministry of Jesus wasn't just to make this process easy, in fact for some people it was far too hard, but it was to make this reconciliation *possible* and achievable. This is what makes the work of Jesus Christ so enduring, even in the minds of people today.

The Gospels finish with the words of John:

Jesus did many other things as well. If every one of them were written down, I suppose that even the whole world would not have room for the books that would be written.

Personally, I have always found this an exaggeration – perhaps it's a deliberate or poetic one. The question that has always concerned me is that if the world were so full of books where would we fit all the people to read them? Surely it's more important to God that people read of the work His Son achieved than creating a repository for books that orbits the Sun at 107,000 kilometres per hour, which is surely too fast for anyone to read them as they zoom by anyway.

The realisation dawns on us that the relative 'little' that has been written is more than we can ever fully take in anyway. The four Gospel records alone have changed lives, societies, civilisations and world history numerous times. The 'little' we have in the story of Jesus has so greatly changed the destiny of humanity that it makes it difficult to comprehend how more books could change us any more!

Yet books on his life continue to be written, yes even this one you are reading now. Is it because there's something missing in the Gospels that needs further examination? There are certainly parts of the story of Jesus that are missing. His life from age twelve to thirty is a notable omission, eighteen out of thirty-three years does seem like a lot. However, there's a deliberateness about Scripture in the way it focuses on his ministry and the four Gospels do not conspicuously differ, although there are a few minor differences in reporting events.

Some recent books seek to analyse the character of Jesus beyond what is represented in the Scriptures (Old and New Testaments). He still provokes curiosity, especially among Gentiles as old-world Hebrews viewed them.

Sometimes these books seek to represent Jesus as a conflicted or complex character. We can probably agree to some extent with conflicted – after all his nature and his mission were evidently difficult. But the Jesus of the Gospels is not complex, for although he certainly had a deep and academic mind, his ministry itself was straightforward and easily understood.

The challenge from the Pharisees regarding the tricky question of money and loyalty is a case in point. Should they pay money to Caesar? Jesus made it simple. He could have taken the argument anywhere; philosophical or esoteric and clearly the Pharisees would have been pleased with an answer that was political. But he didn't pursue a complicated line, he simply said, *"give back to Caesar what is Caesar's"* – it's his money, if he wants it back give it to him!

The core of the Gospel message itself is a simple one – for everyone. Whilst the life of Jesus may be one that on some levels takes a lifetime or more to absorb, his message itself remains simple. His great achievement was that he made it not just simple but relevant – relevant to people - *all* people.

The Gospel itself was first preached to Abraham:

The Apostle Paul wrote that, *Scripture foresaw that God would justify the Gentiles by faith, and announced the gospel in advance to Abraham:* "**All nations will be blessed** *through you.*"

Abraham himself was 'a gentile', called by God from Chaldea. In modern parlance, Abraham was an Iraqi. Moses (who was himself born in Egypt) refers to Abraham's grandson Jacob saying *'My father was a wandering Aramean'*. These men were called to the same Gospel that Jesus, their great descendant, was to preach so many years later.

We could take up the story of Jesus' message from anywhere in his life. His ministry has a wonderful flow to it that can just as easily reach backwards as point forward and we still never lose context or importance. Our purpose is to look at his ministry in its simplicity but also in its diversity; we want to understand the message and its relevance to everyone.

To this end we will consider only a brief period from his life that on a cursory glance looks like much of the rest of his ministry. But there are differences and profound lessons from his life. These few cameos within the Gospels themselves, of the Saviour of the world, changed the lives of the people who were touched by him and his message.

This is Jesus' northernmost ministry - this is Jesus among the Gentiles.

A CLEAN HEART

At the beginning of Christ's northern ministry we take up the narrative from Mark Chapter 7. At this time we find that the Lord Jesus Christ is at least two years through his ministry. He is beginning a year of intense opposition in the lead-up to his crucifixion instigated by the Jewish leaders ultimately carried out by the Roman rulers in the Land.

We find that the Pharisees and lawyers confront him in the town of Gennesaret which is on the Sea of Galilee. They are somewhat pursuing him as it were, whereas in the past they've been content to cross philosophical swords with him whenever he's been near their circles of influence.

Here they challenge him over Jewish tradition, in particular the ritual washing of hands, *"Why don't your disciples live according to the tradition of the elders instead of eating their food with defiled hands?"*

To these elders it wasn't a simple matter of taking exception to the disciples not washing their hands in the sense of hygiene which the disciples had probably done anyway.

The Oral Tradition they observed went far beyond what was sensible for hygiene purposes and also far more than what the Law of Moses instructed. Worse still, these laws were designed *to be seen to be done* so as to make one look pious and holy. This Oral Tradition (from the first fall of Jerusalem to around the times of the Maccabees), eventually became *collated* many centuries later (around 200AD) as the Mishnah. In the time of Jesus however, it was still only an oral tradition.

The Mishnah has six orders (broad-ranging sections) dealing with regulations for almost every facet of daily life:

> Zeraim (Seeds)
> Moed (Festivals)
> Nashim (Women)
> Nezikin (Damages)
> Kodeshim (Holies)
> Tehorot (Purities)

The first part of Tehorot, called *Keilim* (vessels) runs to thirty chapters! After this you can move on through the other sections of Tehorot. *Yadayim* which is section 11 deals with the washing of hands. Having informed oneself of these laws one can move on to *Uktzim* (stems), the final section which only runs to three chapters deals with stems and peels of various fruits and vegetables, whether they are clean or unclean, such as; *A sprig of a vine when stripped of its grapes is clean, but if one grape alone is left thereon it is unclean (unless the remaining grape is a hand's breadth from the end of the stem, in which case it is clean).*

And that is just a sample of these interpretive traditions found in the Mishnah!

Many years have passed since the lawyers of Jesus' day practised this washing of hands, but the Hebrews have proved remarkably accurate in preserving traditions! Here are the instructions for today's *Netilat Yadayim* ('washing of the hands'):

> 1. Clean your hands. You must first make sure your hands are clean, as the purpose of *netilat yadayim* is not cleaning your hands, but rather purifying them.
>
> 2. Take a washing cup, preferably with two handles. Having a cup with two handles will allow you to easily pass the cup from one hand to the other.
>
> 3. Fill the cup while holding the cup with your dominant hand.
>
> 4. Pour the water over your hands. Alternate washing hands two or three times.
>
> 5. While holding your hands in front of you, say the following blessing: (said in Hebrew of course) "Blessed are you, Adonai, our God, King of the universe, who sanctifies us with his commandments, and commanded us regarding washing the hands."
>
> 6. Completely dry your hands with a clean towel.
>
> 7. From this point until you eat the bread, all speaking is forbidden. If you do speak, you must wash again. It is permitted to motion to others for whatever reason.

8. Make the blessing for the bread: "Blessed are you, Adonai, our God, King of the universe, who brings bread from the land."

9. Take a bite of the bread as soon as you finish the blessing.

This was the type of oral tradition that came into contrast with the simple Gospel message Jesus taught! No wonder they didn't like him much – he was breaking their rules. It didn't matter that they were not God's rules, they were rules nonetheless.

The Pharisees are quite up front with their expectations; they don't pretend a Scriptural law is being broken by the disciples – but cunningly they don't specify that they're not either. Instead they want to know why *they* don't follow the tradition of the elders.

Notice that they don't challenge Jesus for doing the same! This was pure trickery on their part. Not only don't they want to be seen to confront him directly - they are making a *slight* that although they may be his disciples, he is not an elder.

What they were trying to do is lure Jesus into an *either-or* situation where he had to admonish his disciples to prove that he was an elder (one with authority). Their game was that if he *didn't* do this he would have declared to everyone that he had no authority (tough call for the Son of God!). But if he *did* admonish them he would have acknowledged the authority of the tradition and by default the Pharisees' authority over him as administrators of traditions and therefore he would be subject to them. It is a tremendously clever manoeuvre on their part.

In my mind I can imagine two expressions on the Lord's face; the first a wry smile in recognition of the craftiness of their trap, and this giving way to a look of intense displeasure at the disregard they had for his Father's Word - replacing it so blithely with their own nonsense. And hence his reply to them:

He replied, "Isaiah was right when he prophesied about you hypocrites; as it is written: 'These people honor me with their lips, but their hearts are far from me. They worship me in vain; their teachings are merely human rules.' You have let go of the commands of God and are holding on to human traditions."

His answer was profoundly simple. He neatly evades their trap with a basic statement that God had never asked for more purification of the hands in addition to cleansing for basic hygiene – if you want to purify something start with your heart!

However, he's not going to let them get away with their trickery so easily. He turns the tables and goes after them on their own turf, citing how they had not only added to God's law – but taken something away from it also – which was a far more serious offence.

"You have a fine way of setting aside the commands of God in order to observe your own traditions! For Moses said, 'Honour

your father and mother,' and, 'Anyone who curses their father or mother is to be put to death.' But you say that if anyone declares that what might have been used to help their father or mother is Corban (that is, devoted to God) - then you no longer let them do anything for their father or mother. Thus you nullify the word of God by your tradition that you have handed down. And you do many things like that."

He was exposing their convenient, tricky little way of setting aside the commandments of God in order to preserve their own traditions.

Ironically this situation came about over a bind these observers of the actual Law of God got themselves into - but soon found a *beautiful* or *fine* way out of! Far from trapping Jesus with their craftiness he out-flanked them, surprising them that he knew not only the whole extent of Scripture but their laws *as well* - including the embarrassing ones!

How the swindle worked was like this: Say a young man cursed his parents, used foul language, embarrassed or debased his parents in the eyes of society – the complete opposite of honouring them. It was up to the elders to put him to death, as simple as that.

Let's just pretend (I say pretend because it would never really happen right?) that a *concerned* elder confronted the young man to ascertain some more information. I mean, you can't just go around stoning young people because they're disrespectful (yes I know what you're thinking, they have no trouble getting stoned by themselves, but let's concentrate on the explanation). And the elder was *just* about to ask the young man a question, when suddenly the young man fell to his knees and with a rather contrite look on his face said, "Out of the goodness of my heart, I have vowed to give God 25% of my wages".

Well what would an elder do? I mean after all, a vow is a very serious matter, one cannot simply deny God what his faithful have vowed to give him. No, vows are serious matters indeed, I mean, it's 'Corban' (*a sacrifice*,) a gift that God is entitled to have, and who am I, a humble elder, to get in the way of what one owes Almighty God?!

Indeed a fine and beautiful way around the problem - wonderfully finessed. Oh, and let's not mention where that 25% of wages went – we wouldn't want to draw attention to who was responsible for the administration of finances relating to how these vows that were duly fulfilled, would we?!

And it didn't take many generations of elders to systemise the fraud. One can imagine how conveniently it not only subverted the Law of God but could be *managed*, manipulated or, God forbid – corrupted! How many elders *only thought* they heard someone dishonour their parents?

Jesus points the finger and exposes them for what they are. They melt away and are not heard from again in the chapter. A hasty retreat is beaten back to the corridors of power and tradition. Clean hands – black hearts.

When the Pharisees had gone, Jesus turns his attention to the people who are gathered in that place and he teaches them, not the complicated, manipulated version of *a* law – but truth in its simplicity:

Again Jesus called the crowd to him and said, "Listen to me, everyone, and understand this. Nothing outside a person can defile them by going into them. Rather, it is what comes out of a person that defiles them."

It's a wonderful contrast that Jesus illustrates. The whole point of *Netilat Yadayim* – the washing of the hands, had nothing to do with what was actually healthy. For the sake of hygiene the hands were already clean *before* the ceremony. The aim of true purification cleansed what? The hands? No, the mind and the heart – the thoughts and the feelings one has.

These come about through habits, by actions, by meditation on what is right and what is wrong. The body is the repository of these things – food is just 'passing through'. What one thinks, and consequently says or does, by these things they are judged in the sight of God.

As the Psalmist wrote, being completely open to God and without qualification or excuse in Psalm 51:

> *Cleanse me with hyssop, and I will be clean;*
> *wash me, and I will be whiter than snow.*
> *Let me hear joy and gladness;*
> *let the bones you have crushed rejoice.*
> *Hide your face from my sins*
> *and blot out all my iniquity.*

> *Create in me a pure heart, O God,*
> *and renew a steadfast spirit within me.*
> *Do not cast me from your presence*
> *or take your Holy Spirit from me.*
> *Restore to me the joy of your salvation*
> *and grant me a willing spirit, to sustain me.*
> *Then I will teach transgressors your ways,*
> *so that sinners will turn back to you.*
> *Deliver me from the guilt of bloodshed, O God,*
> *you who are God my Savior,*
> *and my tongue will sing of your righteousness.*
> *Open my lips, Lord,*
> *and my mouth will declare your praise.*
> *You do not delight in sacrifice, or I would bring it;*
> *you do not take pleasure in burnt offerings.*
> *My sacrifice, O God, is a broken spirit;*
> *a broken and contrite heart*
> *you, God, will not despise.*

Ezekiel wrote along the same lines in Chapter 36. Here are just a couple of verses to whet your appetite:

I will sprinkle clean water on you, and you will be clean; I will cleanse you from all your impurities and from all your idols. I will give you a new heart and put a new spirit in you; I will remove from you your heart of stone and give you a heart of flesh. And I will put my Spirit in you and move you to follow my decrees and be careful to keep my laws.

Jesus' brief explanation to the people aroused the appetite of the disciples to understand more: *After he had left the crowd and entered the house, his disciples asked him about this parable.*

I can imagine this frustrated Jesus a little. I know he had a lot of patience, especially for his disciples but the fact that they had taken his words to be a parable, merely a saying that wasn't meant to be understood literally, may have disappointed him.

"Are you so dull?" he asked. *"Don't you see that nothing that enters a person from the outside can defile them? For it doesn't go into their heart but into their stomach, and then out of the body."*

A small synopsis of the digestive system perhaps. What he meant was that all the things we eat *bypass* the heart, they are just passing through. While the Law of Moses defined some dietary guidelines it had a larger, more important message. And Jesus was foreshadowing the removal of these laws because there was a New Law coming – one that demanded more from the heart.

He went on: "What comes out of a person is what defiles them. For it is from within, out of a person's heart, that evil thoughts come—sexual immorality, theft, murder, adultery, greed, malice, deceit, lewdness, envy, slander, arrogance and folly. All these evils come from inside and defile a person."

That's not a very nice list! But they all come from the heart, which was the seat of feelings, the place where selfishness and self-centredness were. What consequence are clean hands compared to all these nasties? Jesus' ministry was to inspire the opposite of all these things and it began with getting the heart right. He knew the heart of man – and he knew the scale of the challenge.

He did not expect to get through to the Scribes and the Pharisees because they had a veil over their eyes. They were not interested in *seeing* and they didn't want to understand. Other people may have understood but did not have an opportunity. Finally, there were his disciples who hadn't had a veil over their eyes, who had all the opportunity to understand and still they didn't get it!

So we can imagine Jesus being frustrated at this. But having got something through to them at least he made a decision, an interesting one. He decided to go on a road trip and he wanted to take them with him. It may not sound like the best way to describe it as the Lord Jesus going on vacation. But in a way it is true.

There are probably a few very good reasons why Jesus has made this decision at this time in his ministry:

1. He needed to move on from the conflict with the Pharisees, to ground himself and remain positive in himself and with his message.
2. He was acutely aware that his ministry will soon end. No doubt this had been brought into sharper focus by the recent demise of his cousin and fellow preacher, John the Baptist.
3. There were still areas of the Land to cover and he'd spent a lot of time around Galilee.
4. He needed to spend travelling time alone with his disciples to regroup and teach them, to equip them with the wisdom they would need for the time when they would take over the ministry he had begun.
5. He would be demonstrating that salvation is not only for the Jews, which is a lesson the disciples would need in the near future.

Gennesaret where he has been is the area west of the Sea of Galilee. Galilee means 'a circuit'. It first appears in the book of Joshua and seems to imply a district, such as one a Judge would *circuit* – which in his travels was exactly what the Lord and righteous Judge was about to do.

The lake itself was known in the Hebrew as *Chinneret'h* – which is where the New Testament name 'Gennesaret' comes from. *Chinneret'h* first appeared way back in the book of Numbers. For those interested in words; it is derived from the Hebrew word, 'to twang'. *Chinneret'h* means 'a lyre or harp'.

Perhaps as he headed off on the journey, the Master glanced back over his shoulder at the shores he was leaving; the shores of the harp, and recalled Psalm 43 penned by his ancestor David, who was a dab hand with the instrument:

> *Vindicate me, my God,*
> *and plead my cause*
> *against an unfaithful nation.*
> *Rescue me from those who are*
> *deceitful and wicked.*

You are God my stronghold.
Why have you rejected me?
Why must I go about mourning,
oppressed by the enemy?
Send me your light and your faithful care,
let them lead me;
let them bring me to your holy mountain,
to the place where you dwell.
Then I will go to the altar of God,
to God, my joy and my delight.
I will praise you with the lyre,
O God, my God.

(My God, my God...)

why, my soul, are you downcast?
Why so disturbed within me?
Put your hope in God,
for I will yet praise him,
my Saviour and my God.
...

A WOMAN ASKS

Leaving that place, Jesus withdrew to the region of Tyre and Sidon.

Jesus and his disciples travelled from Gennesaret, which is on the north-west shore of the Sea of Galilee and walked towards Tyre and Sidon. That may not sound like a big deal but it is a very long way – especially on foot.

Just to summarize the whole trip: Jesus went from Gennesaret to Tyre and then on to Sidon, we later read that he passed through the *coasts* of the district of Decapolis. He had actually gone west out to the Mediterranean Sea up to Tyre, then continued up the coast to Sarepta, which is the New Testament word for Zarephath and on to Sidon. Then from there we read that, *Jesus left the vicinity of Tyre and went through Sidon, down to the Sea of Galilee and into the region of the Decapolis.*

Going through Sidon to the Sea of Galilee via Decapolis is really like saying that if you are in Adelaide, you will go to Melbourne via Sydney. It is a long way out of your way. It's not the opposite direction but it's certainly not very direct! Or if you are living in Bristol, you will travel to London via Liverpool. Or if you need the U.S. version you head from Washington to New York via Cleveland. It is miles out of the way, especially when we consider that on other occasions he had simply taken a boat straight across Lake Galilee.

Although it does not say specifically that he went right *into* Sidon, he arrived close to the outskirts of the city at least. From there they went down through the passes under Mount Lebanon, probably across the southern foothills of Mount Hermon and down along the coast on the *eastern* side of the Sea of Galilee into the area of Decapolis.

Just to give us an idea of what this distance means: It is about 60km (or 40 miles) from Gennesaret to Tyre and from there another 40km up to Sidon. Then to come back into the closest area of Decapolis, not even into the more populated area, is a return of at least another 120km. So Jesus completed a 220 kilometre or 140 mile hike with the 12 disciples!

As we can see it wasn't just a wander around the corner or a little walk in the park - it was quite some distance and effort that the Lord Jesus made. On this particular trip there were just three events recorded.

But like so many instances in the Scripture there are the *unsaid* things that are not described that make us think. Such as what was it like to walk all that way? What did they talk about? Can we place ourselves in the sandals of the disciples? What was it really like to be on the road with Jesus Christ for a 220km walk? It was a long way and they did not use motorbikes, automobiles, donkeys, tour buses, sports cars or high speed train – they travelled *on foot*.

Can we imagine what it would be like for 13 men walking as one? Or maybe not as one - maybe Philip was walking a little faster than Andrew, or Matthew was always the one trailing behind and John used to like to stop and sit down. We do not know what this trek was like in reality but we can imagine what it would be like to be with these 13 close friends trekking over such a long distance together.

And so Jesus and his disciples reach their first destination and:

He entered a house and did not want anyone to know it; yet he could not keep his presence secret.

We don't know of the connection with this particular house, it was likely the house of a friend or an acquaintance. Maybe it belonged to someone like Jairus, a wealthy ruler who may have had more than one house and who was a good friend to Jesus who had healed his daughter and spent some time with him in Capernaum. Perhaps it was on a recommendation of someone who wanted to extend hospitality to Jesus and so he was able to enter into this house. Or it may have been the house of a family member. One final option is this was just a house, a normal dwelling such as a boarding house where people could come and stay.

So we find him in this house, unlike other places that Lord Jesus has been which seem for the most part to be *outside*. In this place he wants to be inside and maybe alone. Perhaps it was a time when he desired peace and quiet, to be able to gather his thoughts, to pray, and, of course, it was the time he wanted to spend instructing his disciples. As we read through these chapters, and particularly this time that he has spent together with his disciples, we can see that they do need his help.

However, venturing outside the house, the time of peace and quiet was short-lived:

In fact, as soon as she heard about him, a woman whose little daughter was possessed by an impure spirit came and fell at his feet. The woman was a Greek, born in Syrian Phoenicia. She begged Jesus to drive the demon out of her daughter.

Little daughter means she was probably five to nine years old. It is the diminutive form for child. If she was any younger or any older than this another word would be used indicating baby or pre-teen (*brefos* or *padeon*, but *thu-gatreon* is used here).

Interestingly there are no instances of the diminutive form for boy used in Scripture - 'young man' appears but this is definitely referring to someone old enough to be making his own decisions.

There is only one other reference where *little daughter* is used, and as you guessed correctly, it is of Jairus' *little daughter*. Reading the record in Mark 5 of this incident, which is meshed in with the healing of the woman who touched his garment (whom Jesus also calls 'daughter', *thu-gartre*). Here an emotional Jairus called her his *little* daughter but Jesus called her damsel (*padeon*) twice as we read she was *a girl of about twelve*. On the occasion he also called her *little lamb* when he said; *Talitha cumi*: 'little lamb, arise.' There's another reference concerning this we will come back to later.

Therefore we have only two references in the New Testament to a little girl - one for a little Hebrew girl and the other for a little Gentile girl.

We read that her mother was a Greek (which simply means Gentile or non-Jewish), and that she was a Syrophenician by nation, or rather by *genos*, kindred. We are given information that she was a Gentile and then specifically that she was Syrophoenician. These were mixed race people who were part Syrian and part Phoenician, or born in the Syrian division of Phoenicia. The significance of this is that many people in this area were of mixed race because there was a lot of trade and commerce and that usually attracts traders and their families from everywhere.

What makes the account of this woman coming to Jesus important was that her own world was a swirling mass of gods and superstitions. At the nexus of Syrian, Persian, Greek and Cilician cultures, together with the free-wheeling Romans wielding the power and control, there was any number of proponents of one deity or another to call on to save her young daughter.

But this woman had an insider's knowledge! There are two clues to this in Matthew's record of the incident. First she begged him; *Lord, Son of David, have mercy on me!* This is not a casual title to call Jesus. One who uses this phrase was either a very lucky genealogist – or she knew the promises made to David! Those promises include learning of and believing in the Messiah.

The second clue as to how much she knew comes from the term Matthew uses when he wrote, *A Canaanite woman from that vicinity came to him.* Mark calls her by a more contemporary idiom describing her kindred. Canaan meant the *low country* west of the spine of hills running through Israel before it was subdued (mostly) by Joshua. At most this area extended to Tyre but not as far as Sidon, so it's *possible* that this woman had lived some of her life in Israel.

Only Matthew uses this word *Canaan* in the New Testament and he only uses it once – so it is difficult to say what he means by calling her *a woman of Canaan*. Without delving into the matter too deeply, there is a little confusion in the translation of this in the New Testament which needs sorting out another time. It arises from the fact that both Matthew and Mark used the term *Canaanite* to describe the Apostle Simon (not Simon Peter, the other one!). Luke instead named him as *Simon called Zelotes*.

Although there is no definitive proof, it is generally thought that Luke was a Gentile. So why does a Gentile call Simon a Zealot, while Jewish writers of the Gospel call him a Canaanite? I believe the answer is a little obscured in translation somehow because in Hebrew the word for 'zeal' is *kana*; i.e. *The **kana** of the LORD Almighty will accomplish this.* Additional confusion is found in that the Greek word *Kananaios* is someone who comes from Canaan, while a *Kanaios* was someone who came from the town of Cana!

Anyway, it's a side matter we don't want to chase down too far – but I do think it worth mentioning for two reasons; one is that the person concerned (Simon) happened to be at this very time present with Jesus and secondly it high-lights the mixture of peoples, places and languages present in the lives of Jesus and the people he was dealing with – especially this Gentile woman who holds fast to her belief that he is the Messiah!

Going back to our second clue here, the other important thing to note is this phrase, *same coasts*, and means a plural district. What is significant about these same coasts? Well they refer to Tyre *and* Sidon and smack bang in between the two cities is a little place called Sarepta! In the Old Testament the town is known as Zarephath. A very significant thing happened at

Zarephath – a young child had a sickness that was so bad that he *grew worse and worse, and finally stopped breathing* but he was miraculously healed by the Hebrew prophet Elijah.

Elijah (*My God is Yah!*) had healed a child here, and here this woman called on the son of David for a miracle. A woman who knew of Messiah and called for mercy just as another distraught mother had hundreds of years earlier. She believes the story of

Elijah, she believes Jesus (*Yah is salvation*) is the son of David and she believes he can heal her little daughter.

This phrase, *'Lord, Son of David, have mercy on me!'* occurs fourteen times throughout the Gospels and at my count, nine of those occasions are *just* prior to Jesus Christ healing someone.

However, *Jesus did not answer a word. So his disciples came to him and urged him, "Send her away, for she keeps crying out after us."*

For some time I found this response from our Lord Jesus quite perplexing. But the nuances soon become obvious – it was actually an amazing scene! Just imagine, Jesus was making his way and not in any particular hurry. This woman followed him, probably screaming at the top of her lungs in desperation and pleading with tears. The disciples observed this – and what were they thinking? Why doesn't he answer her? If she gets any louder the Romans are going to turn up, I mean there's a whole lot more of them around busy trading ports than the sleepy hollow back at Gennesaret. Other people gathered because humans are curious creatures and are drawn to a rowdy scene.

Jesus knew *exactly* what he was doing.

He was sure of the outcome. In the meantime this woman was doing a whole lot of voluntary preaching for him – not even the disciples were doing that! They asked him earnestly, *"Send her away, for she keeps crying out after us."*

Not quite the *us* they thought; she was actually crying after *him*. And perhaps that in part is the reason for his reply to his disciples, *"I was sent only to the lost sheep of Israel."*

It is assumed the woman heard this. We don't really know because it appears he is just answering the disciples. But the fact that he was talking at all gave this woman hope. Hence she came to him and worshiped him, no longer crying loud and long but pleading, *"Lord, help me."*

Maybe she had heard him. Were those words *lost sheep of the house of Israel* that she heard? Did Peter, James and John hear the same and remember those earlier words of healing; *little lamb, arise.*

Lord, help me. How many times have we said these words? How many times have we been moved by life's circumstances to utter in desperation and faith as this woman did; *Lord, help me*? I don't think we understand well enough the strength that is from above and I don't mean some artificial spirit possessed or metaphorical means of strength – I mean the strength that it takes to have humility, to feel our own humanity and to remain absolutely, resolutely convinced and hold fast that fully-assured-in-faith kind of strength.

Here was a Gentile, a mixed Syrophenician, a woman in a world dominated by men of cunning trade and brutal authoritarian politics – and there's nowhere safer or more assuring for her than at the feet of a man who knew just where she was emotionally. A man who had the same likeness of experience but the total conviction of strength that would take him to the cross, the tomb and a glorious resurrection. *During the days of Jesus' life on earth, he offered up prayers and petitions with fervent cries and tears to the one who could save him from death, and he was heard because of his reverent submission.*

His answer to her plea of *'Lord, help me'* is nothing if not memorable; *"First let the children eat all they want,"* he told her, *"for it is not right to take the children's bread and toss it to the dogs."*

If you have read this before and have wondered how harsh his answer sounds, you'd not be the first or the only one to think so. On the surface it certainly seems so out of character for Jesus. But it is in fact a wonderful challenge to lift our minds spiritually.

This woman is not your average Gentile; Jesus knows she is not an ordinary person who busies herself with only the menial – she is aware of spiritual matters. To some degree we might almost conclude she is a class above what even the disciples could spiritually rise to at this stage.

Look at the words here because we'll learn they are not quite so severe: *Let the children* (or *let the off-spring*) are important because they had a very significant role to play in what this woman achieved with Christ and what he was teaching his disciples. He said: *Let the off-spring, first be filled - for it is not for me* (but it would be for others – and they are standing right here!) *to take the children's bread* and the word means the *whole* loaf, a flat loaf of bread as was commonly baked - and to *throw it* (think Frisbee!) to the dogs. The word dogs is very interesting because it is not the word *kyon* but the word *kynarion* which means little dogs, and can also mean puppies. Again a diminutive word features!

Just to paraphrase what Jesus said to her: *Let the off-spring first be filled for it is not for me to take the children's loaf and throw it to the puppies.* That would be a fairly accurate transliteration of what Jesus actually meant.

We will read of Jesus Christ entering the area of Decapolis, originally part of the area of East Manasseh but had largely been uninhabited by the Hebrew population since their return from Babylon. It was almost exclusively a Gentile area at that time. When he got to the area of Decapolis he repeats his miracle of feeding the 5000 and he fed 4000 people who were mainly Gentiles. So it *was* in the Lord's mind to feed Gentiles. At the feeding of 4000 the *people ate and were satisfied,* they were *filled!* Then they took up the broken pieces left over seven baskets full.

So we read *let the off-spring first be filled* – and then we read a short time later of the Gentiles being filled *anyway*. So he was obviously saying this to test the woman, to draw her out - and she wasn't going to give up.

Far from tormenting her, it was a spiritual and intellectual exchange between two bright minds. Some of this may have been going over the disciples' heads – but it was educational and they would come back to it both in their ministries and epistles. I dare say the Lord was enjoying the exchange somewhat more than one he'd recently had with the Pharisees!

Thus she answers him: *"Lord... even the dogs under the table eat the children's crumbs."*

This woman had seized on Jesus' word *'first'*. So she said, 'OK; if you feed the child first; then can I take the little pluckings that fall, please?' Again, the words are very interesting - she has cleverly changed a couple of them. She said: 'Yes, Lord. The puppies (she steals *his* word!) under the table eat of the children's crumbs.' But then *she* changed *his* word for children. It was not the word for off-spring (commonly used of a son, a male), instead she makes use of the same word that was used to describe the damsel Jesus raised! How much did this woman know?

Jesus originally said a whole loaf of bread should not be given to the puppies - and now she says, 'What about these little crumbs? A female child clumsily drops them from the table and is the puppy not allowed to eat what the children no longer can?' It was a very well-put question.

The irony would not have been lost on the mind of Jesus, whether this woman was playing it or not; for it was Elijah who asked the woman from Zarephath for a *morsel* (a small piece) of bread!

This woman had great faith to be able to press the son of David. This interaction between Jesus and this woman was very important and the disciples were witnessing it.

The further we consider this interaction between Jesus and the woman, the more we see a view of spiritual thought that makes us truly wonder how much this dear lady knew. Had she heard that he had said that *he* was the bread of life? Did she know that he had healed Jairus' daughter? Had she heard of the feeding of the 5,000? Had she been there? Had she heard or seen the Son of God before?

To this woman, one crumb was important; it was all she wanted. When we read of the feeding of the 5,000 and the 4,000 there was bread left over – not just crumbs but bread, whole chunks of bread. This woman asked for only one crumb. This wasn't small for her – it was huge, it was everything, such was her faith.

As I write this section, it happens to be Sunday. At communion this morning I took a piece of bread and held it in my hands. It was more than a crumb but not more than a fragment. It was not huge but to me it was and is *everything*. To this woman, and this is very important, one crumb from the bread of life had more than enough power to grant her petition. It just sinks in when we understand our position and come to petition our Heavenly Father through our Lord Jesus Christ. One crumb from the Bread of Life is more than enough to grant a petition – he has *already* given life itself.

Jesus recognized this in her and he said; *"Woman, you have great faith! Your request is granted."*

This reminds me of that quote in Romans: *For I am not ashamed of the gospel, because it is the power of God that brings salvation to everyone who believes: first to the Jew, then to the Gentile. For in the gospel the righteousness of God is revealed - a righteousness that is by faith from first to last, just as it is written: "The righteous will live by faith."*

In this record of the woman who asked, there is an intriguing little postscript: *She went home and found her child lying on the bed, and the demon gone.*

Again, dwell a little on the unsaid – did she thank Jesus? Of course she did; she believed every word he said, she knew her daughter would be well. Did she linger to share an insight or two with this band of travellers from Galilee? No, she took leave as soon as politeness would permit and ran home to her beloved child.

Standing there, watching her go, a tear may have coursed down the face of Jesus. His humanity and in his compassion he would have imagined the beautiful reunion of mother and daughter and this would have moved him immensely. I can imagine the disciples watching her go too, having learned a little more of how the Master changed people, their lives and their hopes.

One woman, a faithful and intelligent woman was rushing home to love and to hold her daughter. These two individuals were not just the 'lucky ones' – no, far from it. They were themselves now the *seed* of the Bread of Life. They were *his* offspring. A faithful woman, one who knew the promises, one who knew of the Messiah, the son of David and believed in him – and *before* he had done anything for her, in healing her daughter. Do you think she would soon forget this miracle? Not likely. Do you think she would have told her daughter who had healed her, who had saved her; who had given her life? Absolutely!

Jesus knew *exactly* what he was doing.

Soon, after he fulfilled his ministry and mission, there would be others. Their names were Paul, Silas, Barnabas, John Mark and other disciples and preachers of the Way. On their way to and from Israel and the Gentile world they would take refuge with faithful brothers and sisters - sisters such as the faithful woman and her daughter in the coasts of Tyre and Sidon.

These travellers for Christ would need shelter, a morsel or two of bread, hospitality and spiritual encouragement – and who better to provide this than faithful sisters, touched by the work of the Master, to provide for them and the ever expanding calling to life?!

Jesus knew *exactly* what he was doing.

Returning briefly to the postscript: *She went home and found her child lying on the bed, and the demon gone.* Just pause a moment and consider the final phrase, I really do think it is important: she *found her child lying on the bed*.

Remember the healing of Jairus' daughter. What happened? Jesus *took her by the hand... Immediately the girl stood up and began to walk around... and [he] told them to give her something to eat.*

This speaks volumes about the real work of Jesus. Just imagine; this woman arrived home and found her daughter alive and laid upon her bed, the tranquillity of the moment juxtaposed with the outpouring of pleading for her healing. It was not Jesus who took her hand and raised her from her place of rest – it was 'the woman who asked'.

Jesus let *her* do it. She was not empowered to heal but she was empowered to *do*. Only this mother could imagine the powerful emotions of what the Master left for *her* to do. Only a man touched with the infirmities of our flesh could grasp the meaning of life so brutally as to be crucified but so tenderly to let that daughter feel the strong and courageous hands of a mother who loved her and had the faith to *ask*.

It would be in but one blink of an eye that this faithful and spiritually intelligent woman of the coasts of Tyre and Sidon had a meal prepared for her daughter – who sat at the table with her, perhaps the puppies expectantly waiting beneath – and shared a morsel.

What a special meal that would have been. What a role model this mother was. What precious lessons would have been passed across that table of fellowship. What inspiration we now have to *do*, to bless and walk in the way we have been shown, whoever we are – and to *ask*.

Because there is one loaf, we, who are many, are one body, for we all share the one loaf.

A MAN SPEAKS

In Scripture we are often given information about a time or an incident – but really, these are only a small part of the *actual* time in which they occur. Such was this time in the ministry of Jesus.

We don't know how long Jesus Christ was in the area around Sidon. We don't know whether he was in that area just for the salvation of this woman and to establish her faith, or for others who observed the event also.

What else Jesus did and what else happened while he was in the area is at best a rough guess. I don't think we can read into Scripture anything that is not there. However, it is important that we think about these 'gaps' because they draw us into the story and allow us to meditate on the lives that are affected, to some extent our own – not that we were there (or needed to be) but because there are lessons in those gaps for us.

One wonders about the experience of the disciples. What other things were seen and done when Jesus and his disciples spent time on the shores of the Mediterranean, or perhaps in the markets and bazaars of old-time Phoenicia. How would this leave an impression on the disciples? Would what they heard and saw on this tour affect their future lives as leading lights in the new community of believers?

For some of them, just being in the area was like visiting a foreign country. We cannot say with any certainty that it was so different that they experienced culture shock – but it really was a different world from the one they were used to. Most of the disciples would have had lifestyles that were 'village based', they (as most of the people in the land) had little need of travel, except perhaps an occasional visit to Jerusalem or to a relative who had married someone from a community nearby. For the most part the people of the Land were occupied with local work and activity.

Such wide-ranging travel was the exception rather than the rule. Peter, Andrew, James and John, all fisherman, would have been amazed with the size and splendour of the huge vessels that plied the Mediterranean compared with the little boats that fished the waters of Galilee. Buildings, colours, languages, customs, food, produce and a whole range of other experiences would have been surprising and new to them.

This rich immersion in culture, together with time spent with Jesus gave them an education necessary, if not yet complete, for the brave new world to which they would take the Gospel. And thus, the work in Sidon was done.

Then Jesus left the vicinity of Tyre and went through Sidon, down to the Sea of Galilee and into the region of the Decapolis.

This too was quite a journey. We often read such simple statements but don't realise how much time or effort these movements from one place to another take. It was not a brief stroll to come down from the coasts of Tyre and Sidon through the midst of the coast of Decapolis.

Average walking speed is around 5km (3 miles) per hour and they travelled about 60km. But the going would have been a little different to our experience; not only was the terrain up and down but the roads were rough compared to what we generally regard as 'roads'. Then there were stops to rest, eat, sleep or ask directions. It probably doesn't serve a useful purpose to estimate how long the expedition took them – but it does help to imagine it.

We can imagine Jesus and the disciples crossing back over the Litani River and coming down into the Huleh Valley and up over the Golan Heights, across another river, perhaps in sight of glorious mountain Hermon as they made their way to Decapolis.

Considering their journey, it's not that they just travelled along the eastern shore of Lake Galilee, instead they went through the heart of the district. The King James Version of the Bible records that they went through the *midst* of the coasts of

Decapolis. So they really went thoroughly through *the region of the Decapolis.*

The Decapolis was a well-established and well-recognised geographical area. Much had happened since this area was known as Eastern Manasseh and the glory days when the Kingdom of Solomon stretched all the way to the Euphrates River. The Assyrians, Babylonians, Persians, Greeks and now the Romans claimed dominion over the area. It was certainly a well-trodden patch of ground.

After Alexander the Great's demise his empire was divided among his four generals: Ptolemy in Israel and Egypt, Cassander in Greece, Lysimachus in Asia Minor and Seleucus ruled Babylon, Persia and the east. Subsequently the kingdom of Seleucus became the Seleucid Empire and Ptolemy's the Ptolemaic Empire. It wasn't long before these two came into conflict and were known to the Prophet Daniel as the King of the North and the King of the South. The shenanigans between the two make interesting foretelling in his eleventh chapter! However, for reason of *trying* to stay on subject we won't explore this right now.

What is important about this history is that the Decapolis was right in the cross-fire of these two behemoth kingdoms. They were Hellenistic in nature, that is they both wanted the whole world to speak Greek, look Greek and generally be Greek if they could. And nowhere was this more obvious than in the Decapolis!

We know that Jesus Christ did not spend his entire life in the Land of Israel. As a child he spent several years in Roman-ruled Egypt but when it came to his ministry this was almost exclusively spent in Israel, a great majority of it in the north around Galilee. But here he is in Roman, Hellenistic, East

Manassen, Decapolis. Deca-polis simply means 'ten cities'. These ten cities were administered by a governor. One of the ten cities was just west of the river Jordan but the rest were on the east side.

The historian Pliny (the Elder) in his tome *'Naturalis Historia'* names these Ten cities as:

Gerasa (Jerash) in Jordan
Scythopolis (Beth-Shean) in Israel,
Hippos (Hippus or Sussita) in Israel
Gadara (Umm Qais) in Jordan
Pella (West of Irbid) in Jordan
Philadelphia, modern day Amman, the capital of Jordan
Capitolias (Dion) (Beit Ras) in Jordan
Canatha (Qanawat) in Syria
Raphana in Jordan
Damascus, in Syria.

The Decapolis

These ten cities were established by either the Ptolemaic or Seleucid empires, hence the Hellenistic names. Particularly under Roman rule from 63BC autonomy in these cities was encouraged, so much so that they even allowed to mint their own coins which of course bore images of Greek, Roman and their local gods.

It was into this area and culture that Jesus and his disciples arrived. He had of course been in this area once before. That was when they crossed Lake Galilee by boat and found on the opposite side, on the shores of the Decapolis, a man by the name of Legion whom he healed. On this occasion; *they came over unto the other side of the sea, into the country of the Gadarenes* – the Gadarenes being inhabitants from Gadara, which was one of the ten cities.

Here the famous healing miracle performed on Legion ended when 2,000 pigs flew off the cliffs into the lake and drowned. Jesus was back in the area he was politely asked to leave from earlier.

However, Legion remained; *and began to tell in the Decapolis how much Jesus had done for him. And all the people were amazed.* Legion, once confined by his illness to living in the tombs of the dead – was now free and roaming the whole of the Decapolis telling everyone about Jesus. Decapolis as we've discovered covers quite an area, it's a large task for one man, perhaps it's telling that the record says he 'began', he had much preaching ahead of him.

So Jesus is back to follow up, as it were, the missionary work of his *disciple* Legion. This time he was welcomed by the people who had heard about him (although some of them may have remained a little unhappy about the price of pork, due to the lack of supply).

For a certain group of friends it was into this atmosphere of readiness to see Jesus, that they *brought to him a man who was deaf and could hardly talk, and they begged Jesus to place his hand on him.*

This man who was brought to Christ was totally deaf - that is he could hear nothing at all. But he was not entirely dumb as he had an impediment in his speech. That is he had some kind of communication, whether by grunts or by growls.

As this man was presented to him Jesus must have contemplated, if only briefly, the juxtaposition of a man who was physically deaf and spoke with an impediment – and the Pharisees who were spiritually deaf and whose speech was an impediment to others!

This man could communicate but not to the point in which he could converse or hold a meaningful conversation with anyone.

We can imagine what it is like to be deaf. We can cover our ears or shut ourselves in a sound-proof place – and we know it to be a disruptive process. The deaf today have much assistance from organizations which help those with such an impediment and technologies have been developed which also make their lives immensely better. But those who were deaf from the time in which the Gospels were written were very much on their own.

We *should* imagine ourselves in the place of this deaf man here. This is not an unreasonable thing to ask because it is in Scripture to enable us to associate so we can draw out spiritual lessons. Imagine what it is like to go to a theatre and not to be able to hear, to go to the shop or bank or work and not converse, or to go to school and only be able to read what is on the blackboard and not hear the teacher.

53

There are inspirational examples of deaf (and dumb) people who have been able to transcend the difficulties of hearing or speech loss – and they are quite amazing people. A good example is perhaps Helen Keller who was blind also.

In this chapter a man was before Jesus who was in his own way shut off from the world. Not able to speak, not able to ask for a drink, to ask for something to eat, or to be able to explain to friends, family or loved ones that he was hungry, hot, cold or uncomfortable - let alone communicate higher thoughts or spiritual matters. I think it was, despite his circumstances, a great credit to this man that he had *friends* who brought him to Jesus. He must have made an enormous effort to interact with others to the point at which they valued him and therefore sought his healing.

Although he was deaf he is not entirely without speech as we have already mentioned. This word *hardly* means *with difficultly* - with great difficulty he could make a noise but it was hard to communicate with any competence.

The same word can be found in a couple of other occasions in Scripture, such as in the Gospel of Luke; *And, lo, a spirit taketh him, and he suddenly crieth out; and it teareth him that he* *foameth again, and bruising him **hardly** departeth from him (KJV)*. We can take this likewise to mean that only with great difficulty this boy was able to extract himself from his convulsions. *Hardly* is the same word used here of the man with a speech impediment.

It is difficult to explain what it is like not to be able to communicate but I actually had an incident in my life some years ago, where for neurological reasons, I lost the power of speech and also the ability to walk. It was a time of concern but also *frustration*.

The terrible fear of not being able to talk or walk again eventually passed as the days progressed and I felt some relief and some progress. I left behind the fear that I would not regain the use of these abilities and concentrated instead on trying to recover.

I remember one day sitting out in the sun with a therapist, who was on one side of the table with her notepad, while I was on my side with my notepad – hers to record professional notes; mine just to write what I ordinarily would be plainly saying.

One thing I couldn't explain even in writing, no matter how hard I tried, was how *frustrating* it was *trying* to speak. So I resorted to an action to describe the feeling. I'll do the same here for you so you can get inside the mind of the man who stood before Jesus too.

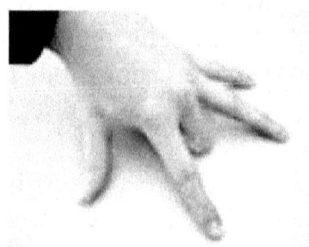

It's called the *Paralyzed Finger Trick*. Take your hand and place it palm down on a flat surface. Now tuck your middle finger underneath so; you should have the knuckle of the back of your middle finger resting on top of the surface.

Now lift your thumb off the surface and hold it there for a second and put it down again. OK, that's easy, right? Now take your little finger and lift it off the surface and just hold it for a second. Still easy to do? Next lift your index finger off the surface and hold it for a second. Still good?

Now try your ring finger.

Difficult, isn't it?! I can't do it at all. That is the meaning of *hardly*, that is the sensation of impediment in this man's speech. I wanted to give you this little exercise because it not only explains the word but it gives you an almost identical *physical feeling* in your own body, an impediment in your own experience. I think you'll agree – it really is frustrating.

And in case you were wondering, yes I regained my ability to walk (I've got short legs so I run everywhere) – and much to the disappointment of my family and friends my ability to converse has never been better!

Back to our story in the Decapolis where the man was likewise frustrated and unable to converse with Jesus. He was locked in his own body, unfit to express himself. He was a bright person. He was an interesting person. He could have a discussion with you about some wonderful things in life, in nature or in the social world. Perhaps had a brilliant sense of humour. He most probably had a kind and giving nature but his problem was that he could not tell anyone and it frustrated him.

Let's stop and ask ourselves a spiritual question for a minute: what is our hearing like? What do we *choose* to hear? Do we listen to silly talk? Do we indulge in listening to blasphemy or misconduct of speech? What do we let *into our* ears?

And how do we use *our* faculty of speech? What do we say to one another? Is what comes from our mind good things, spiritual thoughts of wisdom, love, kindness, of depth of character - or are these thoughts shallow and unappreciative? Only we can answer this, only we can change and improve these.

But that is why we read of a deaf man brought to Jesus, so that 2,000 years later we can ask just such questions. This is what we are meant to see and these are the questions we are meant to ask. These are the things that we are challenged to address in our times as we consider the life, ministry and example of our Lord Jesus right back there in Scripture.

After he took him aside, away from the crowd, Jesus put his fingers into the man's ears. Then he spit and touched the man's tongue. This stands out as a most unusual healing process. We can see in each of these actions that Jesus Christ was using means *other than* speech and hearing to communicate with this man.

Perhaps Jesus knew what this man would be like and that is why it is recorded for us. It may be that he was a person who is later mentioned in the Acts of the Apostles, in the Gospels or Epistles because he became a faithful disciple. Jesus saw him and recognized in him someone who needed *more* than just healing.

On occasions when people could hear, Jesus challenged these people also. To blind men he asked, *'Do you believe that I am able to do this?'* and to another; *'What do you want me to do for you?'* It was always part of his process and method to draw people out of themselves, to express themselves.

When it came to the deaf man he used this relevant method. He took him aside or singled him out from the multitude. Then he put his fingers in his ears because he had to tell the man that he knew of his deficiency and that what he was about to do concerned his ears.

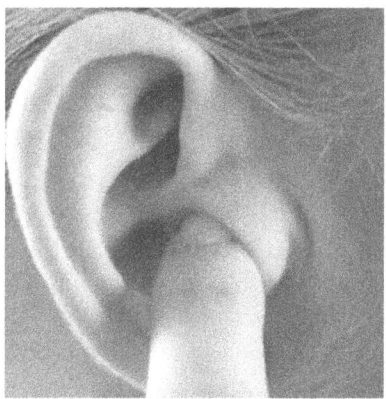

Just imagine being in that man's sandals - imagine what it would be like not to hear a thing, to be in total silence and stand there looking into the face of the Son of God. Imagine that!

So Jesus reached out to him with hands not yet pierced with the nails of his suffering, kind hands that had touched and healed so many already. The man saw the hands coming closer to his face, around his head, and then he felt the fingers in his ears. He stood there looking straight into eyes of the Lord Jesus Christ, facing him and waiting. What an awesome experience, imagine how the man would later recall that moment – the image of the only begotten son of God indelibly etched in his memory forever.

Still looking intently, Jesus removed his fingers from the man's ears, spat on one and reached out his finger towards the man's mouth. The man was transfixed, his mouth already open in surprise, and he felt the Lord touch his tongue.

Everything was done so deliberately. There was no simple 'go thy way, for thou art healed', Christ had healed from a distance before – in fact he'd just done so for the Syrophenician woman's daughter. Others had touched him and been made whole. But for this man the treatment was different. His world was silent, he'd heard nothing of Jesus (or anyone for that matter) and since his friends had brought him to be healed we assume he hadn't been following the Lord's ministry with the only sense he had, his sight.

So with these actions Jesus was reaching across a barrier through touch and a visual process to teach the man to trust and believe him.

Spitting in the Old Testament was almost always a sign of shame and we read in the Gospels that it was likewise used to shame Christ when he was spat on. However, on the three occasions he did so himself it was always for healing or for good. In the Old Testament the finger was used in worship, to cleanse and to purify offerings and temple equipment. Here it was the saliva of Christ on the tongue of the dumb to heal and teach this man faith.

Imagine the sensation; if someone sticks a finger in your ear you can feel it for ages afterwards. My mischievous little sister has an annoying habit of licking her finger, sneaking up behind the unsuspecting and sticking her finger in their ear – then running away shrieking with laughter. You shudder at the sensation for days! Unfortunately, I fear the practice is being passed on to her children.

So this man with the touch of the master still in his ears and on his tongue, fresh on his senses, looked on intently.

It is not enough to touch the Master, but to be touched by him. In his healing Jesus used touch to *emphasise* faith. The Syrophenician woman's faith had healed her daughter, the Centurion's faith had healed his servant – their faith in him made the miracle complete. For others more direct intervention was required.

Similarly today, there are many who know of Jesus, who have a head-knowledge of him but remain untouched, un-moved by his teaching. Some remain so through neglect, others such as this deaf man, merely by his ignorance. But Jesus was drawing him out, showing him with the senses that he did possess, those of sight and touch, that he could have faith.

He looked up to heaven and with a deep sigh said to him, "Ephphatha!" (which means "Be opened!"). The man had sight, he could see the Lord Jesus. He had just had Jesus' fingers in his ears and then his finger upon his tongue and now he looked on absolutely fascinated as this communication was working out.

His face was fixed on Jesus, then he saw him look up to Heaven. What happens when somebody else looks up? You do the same thing! Particularly if they look up and point and have an urgent expression on their face - you always look up.

The man saw Jesus look up calmly and he wondered what he was looking at. Or did he? Perhaps the man saw that up there somewhere was hope and he realised that now he was going to receive the gift of hearing and the gift of speech. Christ looked up and so did the deaf man and then looking back down again he saw Jesus sigh. He did not hear it, he just *saw* Jesus' shoulders slump and his chest contract as air from his lungs came out in a long sigh.

Why did Jesus sigh? It seems such an odd little action compared with the drama of sticking his fingers in someone's ears and pronouncing a dramatic word. These are just such actions that draw our attention – and that is why he did it. It could be that he was feeling the same sensation he did when the woman with the issue of blood touched him and he *perceived that virtue had gone out of him*. He was after all the one who took our infirmities upon himself.

Surely he took up our pain and bore our suffering... he was oppressed and afflicted... he was led like a lamb to the slaughter, and as a sheep before its shearers is silent, so he did not open his mouth.... he poured out his life unto death; this is enough to make anyone sigh.

One scholar ventures that Jesus was sighing because he knew what new temptations this man would face with the ability to hear evil and speak amiss - both are great challenges for those of us with ears to hear and a tongue to speak. Although there is probably some practical recognition for this I think there is more to it.

Jesus probably had many thoughts concerning the significance of what he was doing. Looking at the poor man, sighing, as he considered his situation; I wonder if Christ recalled the words of his Father to Moses at the bush. *The LORD said to him, "Who gave human beings their mouths? Who makes them deaf or mute? Who gives them sight or makes them blind? Is it not I, the Lord? Now go; I will help you speak and will teach you what to say."*, - imagine Jesus thinking at that point as he touched the man's tongue - *Now therefore go, and I will be with thy mouth, and teach thee what thou shalt say.*

Perhaps he sighed as an expression of pity or frustration. Looking into the face of the man as to whether he might be better off deaf and dumb and walk to the Kingdom with less to hear, less to say, less reason to bridle the tongue or stop the ears.

Perhaps the Lord Jesus Christ wondered what this man would hear and what he would say. I cannot speak for you but should I put myself in that deaf and dumb man's place I can well and truly imagine the Lord sighing with despair, for in me he'd have seen a whole lot of trouble!

You might expect me to quote here what is said in the Epistle of James about bridles and tongues. Instead, I think Psalm 39 speaks more eloquently on this. Surely the Lord Jesus reflected on this Psalm at some time:

> *I said, "I will watch my ways*
> *and keep my tongue from sin;*
> *I will put a muzzle on my mouth*
> *while in the presence of the wicked."*
> *So I remained utterly silent,*

not even saying anything good.
But my anguish increased;
my heart grew hot within me.
While I meditated, the fire burned;
then I spoke with my tongue:
"Show me, Lord, my life's end
and the number of my days;
let me know how fleeting my life is.
You have made my days a mere handbreadth;
the span of my years is as nothing before you.
Everyone is but a breath,
even those who seem secure.
"Surely everyone goes around like a mere phantom;
in vain they rush about, heaping up wealth
without knowing whose it will finally be.
"But now, Lord, what do I look for?
My hope is in you.
Save me from all my transgressions;
do not make me the scorn of fools.
I was silent; I would not open my mouth,
for you are the one who has done this.
Remove your scourge from me;
I am overcome by the blow of your hand.
When you rebuke and discipline anyone for their sin,
you consume their wealth like a moth—
surely everyone is but a breath.
"Hear my prayer, Lord,
listen to my cry for help;
do not be deaf to my weeping.
I dwell with you as a foreigner,
a stranger, as all my ancestors were.
Look away from me, that I may enjoy life again
before I depart and am no more."

Such is the condition in which humanity finds itself. The Lord Jesus, acutely aware of this state, remained resolute in his life, not allowing the frailty of the flesh to eclipse the hope of eternity.

Then back to the man who was looking into the eyes of Christ once again, he saw the words formed on his mouth *"Ephphatha"*. He had probably done his fair share of lip reading. Just say that word slowly to yourself and notice the actions of your mouth and in particular that of your tongue. It is pronounced 'ef-fath-ah', try it.

Ephphatha is an Aramaic word derived from the Hebrew word 'pathakh' which means to be open, to be free or to shake yourself loose.

Another little thing to notice is that there is a translation given in the verse: *that is, be opened*. But someone who knew this word would soon pick up the difference in the translation in Mark! Ephphatha doesn't simply mean 'be opened' - it means 'be *thou* opened'.

Christ was not just telling the ears to open and the tongue to loose itself – he was telling the owner of these to be open! To accept him as the Christ, the son of God by whose power he was able to hear the Gospel and to then praise with all that was in because he was whole in all his senses!

At this, the man's ears were opened, his tongue was loosened and he began to speak plainly. As soon as the word was uttered the air about the man was suddenly filled with sound. A bird in the distance, the murmuring of the multitude. Perhaps he heard gasps, or the shuffling footsteps of his friends and the disciples in the gravel. He'd be looking to see where each new sound was coming from. Just moments before he was transfixed and following the actions of Jesus, now his head was darting every which way, homing in on where each new sound came from. He'd gone from stunned mullet to feature animation!

Immediately, suddenly the string of his tongue was loosed as if it had been rolled up, tied with string like roast lamb because this phrase means it was as if his tongue was tied up in his mouth. You know what it is like to be tongue-tied or to do a tongue twister. I gave you an example before about what is it like to feel this frustration *tied-up* in your own body. Now he is liberated.

Suddenly, there was remarkable freedom and he spoke *plainly*. He did not need to be taught how to speak as most people who make a modest or full recovery - he could speak plainly immediately. What a glorious *relief* to be able to express himself like that!

There are many little things that frustrate us. You know what it is like to forget where you have put something. Where are my glasses? All the time walking around with them on your head. I can't remember some things written in the Scripture, and I often become so frustrated because I want to return to the passage and show someone that gem I saw just this morning.

In this life not everything is easy or possible because our abilities or mental faculties have not yet been freed and this is the spiritual story that is sent down through the ages in this man's situation - we *too* are frustrated and *we* need to look into the face of him who wants us to be saved.

> *Strengthen the feeble hands,*
> *steady the knees that give way;*

say to those with fearful hearts,
"Be strong, do not fear;
your God will come,
he will come with vengeance;
with divine retribution
he will come to save you."
Then will the eyes of the blind be opened
and the ears of the deaf unstopped.
Then will the lame leap like a deer,
and the mute tongue shout for joy.
Water will gush forth in the wilderness
and streams in the desert.

Yes, even in the midst of Decapolis

When we are weak – he is strong. When we are feeble – he is able. When we are fearful – he is ready to comfort. That is Christ's representative work, the other side of his mediatorship.

Jesus commanded them not to tell anyone. But the more he did so, the more they kept talking about it. The man's friends were delighted, they were so happy they'd made the decision to bring their friend to him. It was they who desired the healing. It was they who brought him to Jesus *in faith* that he would heal him. And now they couldn't stop talking about it!

There are several occasions in the Gospel records where Jesus gave instructions after performing miracles. When he healed a leper he told him; *'See that you don't tell this to anyone. But go, show yourself to the priest and offer the sacrifices that Moses commanded for your cleansing, as a testimony to them.'* No one ever recovered from leprosy. The cleansing ceremony the priest performed would have been a first for him as well as the healed leper! It was a remarkable testimony of Christ's power to heal.

But in this instance, to the deaf and dumb man and his friends, the instruction is given, *'See that you don't tell this to anyone'*. Why did Jesus say this? There were thousands of people following him, many had just seen what he'd done, they didn't need to hear about it second-hand.

It appears difficult from just examining Scripture itself to ascertain why he didn't want his miracles 'broadcast' as it were. Some scholars tentatively suggest he didn't want to be known simply as a miracle worker, others that he did miracles out of humility only, some think that he had a fear of attention from the authorities of the day, Jewish or Roman.

While there may be an element of truth to these suggestions, of themselves they're not really convincing arguments – certainly not any which satisfy a curious mind!

Jesus *did* want miracles known because they were tangible evidence of the authority he had from God. He performed miracles *openly* such as feeding thousands at a time. He was a humble man but he wasn't going to hide his light under a bushel. As for fear of authoritarian attention, not only did he receive plenty of that on many occasions, he was more than prepared to go through with the consequences – and did so right through his crucifixion. He wasn't *scared* of the authorities.

There is one idea however that does make some sense of his instruction and it's not found in the minutiae of his actions, but rather by stepping back and considering the big picture. He came into this world to save it, not en masse but by *personal* salvation – his ministry was not to save ears, eyes and limbs but whole lives.

In the case of the deaf and dumb man he wanted him to go away with the Gospel message, not just a story about healing. Healing is a small matter when weighed against eternal salvation. If the miracle was the focus instead of the Gospel then the receiver was in danger of losing 'real' sight of salvation.

Jesus is the Messiah and today that still has *mass appeal*. But he didn't (and doesn't!) call crowds to salvation – he converts everyone individually and personally. Even today the call of the Gospel is heard one by one. One here, one there, each called and every one known personally to him. He knows our names, our personalities, our characters, our hearts, minds and our habits (good and bad).

Those that were sick, lame, blind, deaf, bleeding, dying who were healed were just that, healed – he wanted more than healing, he wanted salvation. And when someone realises this and they want to share this amazing message, it's not going to be achieved by yelling it out in the town square - but in the quietude of sitting down with a friend and telling them of the Gospel and how the miracle proves it. And one by one, in the Lord's way, another will come to him.

Perhaps the second part of the answer is found in what we recognise today as 'celebrity syndrome'. This not only applied to the stardom the society of that day wanted to lumber Jesus with, thus detracting from the message instead of reinforcing it – but also to those he healed.

We know well from the media of today how Siamese twins are treated when separated, or face-transplant patients, or celebrity cancer survivors – they are put upon by the media baying for scraps of information to feed the curious masses. That's not rich ground for the Gospel, that's dry ground, stony ground, wayside ground – Jesus is seeking to protect them from the perils that *broadcasting* the Gospel in this way can bring.

Human nature being what it is, the friends of the deaf and dumb man thought this advice less than compelling so they did as they pleased; *the more he did so, the more they kept talking about it.*

What would you have done? I know I'd probably need the whole instruction explained in more detail, drummed into me, be made to repeat it several times and then write it out a hundred times on the blackboard before the reality of it dawned on me too. After all, for them it was the most amazing thing that had happened all year – even in cosmopolitan Decapolis.

People were overwhelmed with amazement. "He has done everything well," they said. "He even makes the deaf hear and the mute speak." 'Overwhelmed with amazement' is a funny little expression. The original text actually comes from two words, *ek* – 'out of', and *plasso* – 'smite or expel by a blow'. In modern parlance they were 'totally blown away' – and that's not far from the actual meaning.

There's a beautiful irony in this chapter that the translation doesn't exactly high-light but is worth consideration. They said he *'has done everything well'* - and this appears like a book-end. It's almost exactly the same phrase that Jesus himself accused the Pharisees of in the beginning of the chapter! The *fine or beautiful way* applied sarcastically to the Pharisees' evil manipulation of the Law – was then applied to Jesus in ecstatic jubilation by the Gentiles for his good work!

Don't tell me Mark didn't have a chuckle as he wrote this down. I simply won't believe you. It's yet another fine and beautiful way Scripture is recorded for our benefit, to recall and understand the mind of the Master who could bravely stare down a corrupt establishment and at the same time, with conviction and good grace, call to salvation those who were otherwise nobodies in the eyes of the world. He certainly was the real deal.

He *has* done everything well – and we are encouraged by his example, Paul sees to this in Corinthians; *When you come together, each of you has a hymn, or a word of instruction, a revelation, a tongue or an interpretation. Everything must be done so that the assembly may be built up… everything should be done in a fitting and orderly way.*

There's a storyline to Paul's words, a narrative – perhaps it's the narrative of the healing of the deaf and dumb. Jesus and the man went together aside from the multitude. The man had a Psalm he couldn't sing. Jesus had a doctrine. The man had a tongue he couldn't use. Jesus had a revelation. In their strained communication there was an interpretation they could both understand and in this there was freedom. There was an order to the healing of the man and that order was edifying – and well done.

If ever there was a doctrine of 'paying it forward' – it's the Gospel. What greater good is there than saving lives? That is the call of Christ to all people, some won't receive it but some will, and those who do he'll praise for hearing and speaking so in his name - **Well done**, *good and faithful servant!... Come and share your master's happiness!*

A MULTITUDE FEED

It appears from the record in Matthew that the healing of the deaf and dumb man had fanned the flames of interest in Jesus and his miracles in the region: *Great crowds came to him, bringing the lame, the blind, the crippled, the mute and many others, and laid them at his feet; and he healed them. The people were amazed when they saw the mute speaking, the crippled made well, the lame walking and the blind seeing. And they praised the God of Israel.*

It would have been interesting to be there with the Lord Jesus Christ when he spoke to the Syrophoenician woman and witnessed the discussion that took place between them. And fascinating also to be in that little knot of faithful friends who brought a deaf man with a speech impediment to Jesus.

But in contrast to these intimate moments with the Lord, whole communities were stirred, so much so that *crowds* – an innumerable mass, were drawn to him. More than this, they are described as 'great' crowds, the biggest adjective is used. In fact it is the same word that is used on many occasions to describe 'many' and 'much' in the sense of plenteous or immeasurable abundance.

That so many were gathered to him in one place in these times was not commonplace. In an age of relatively localized travel, with no modern forms of transport, finding so many people in one place for a reason other than war or radical civil unrest was very unusual.

It is nothing for us to imagine fifty thousand or more gathered for a sporting event, all paying patrons of course. But for thousands to gather and mill around just to catch a glimpse of one extraordinary man who was making people well – that is not something that we can readily relate to.

We have to understand the dynamics of life in the times that the disciples were writing about. There were no large cities nearby, not like we know today. Even Jerusalem only had a population of somewhere between thirty to fifty thousand, depending on feast times throughout the year. The cities of the Decapolis were smaller; the agrarian nature of the area and the fertility of the geography probably meant that these cities could support a population much less than others. So a great multitude coming together as described was a miracle in itself!

From the cities, towns and villages of the Decapolis, little lines of people emerged. Their lines formed up as they crossed the fields and the rolling vales: somewhere in the district of Decapolis was this man Jesus. The voices of one small caravan to another would convey the messages of the travellers:
"He is in such a place."
"My friend said he was in Canatha yesterday."
"He was seen in Dion recently and healed a blind woman there."

And so the lines would follow the rumours through the area, the young and the old, the maimed, lame, blind, deaf, dumb, diseased and the lost. All had heard, all hoped for the rumours, the fame of the man of Galilee to be true, to be real, to be nearby.

There were men and women carrying sick and crying children, teenagers rollicking and chasing each other as the multitudes carried themselves forward. A blind man called for someone to lead him, a lame man leant on the arm of a friend as they stumbled forward. The crowds followed, these Gentiles, a milling, moving mass – to see, to hear, to touch Jesus of

Nazareth, the man from the other side; the man of miracles and hope.

And so it was one day they found him. We are not told where, however we know that he was travelling through the area rather than just wandering around it and had come down from the north. He had healed a deaf and dumb man somewhere. Now a few days later he was still making his way down through the Decapolis in a clockwise direction towards the southeast of the Sea of Galilee. Since this was the second major event in his movement through the area and speculating on the time of year and the other events in his life when he passed back into the area of Galilee, it is reasonable to estimate he was in middle to lower Decapolis, perhaps in the area of Raphana or near the River Yarmuk – in a wilderness place.

And it was in this place that Jesus chose to linger for a while, not from weariness, but because the situation called for a miracle. *During those days another large crowd gathered. Since they had nothing to eat, Jesus called his disciples to him and said, "I have compassion for these people; they have already been with me three days and have nothing to eat. If I send them home hungry, they will collapse on the way, because some of them have come a long distance."*

There was always a reason, another aspect to a miracle or even a word from Jesus. From a casual consideration of his ministry it may seem as if he just wandered around doing things here and there as he felt like it. Knowledge of the prophecies about Jesus reveal otherwise but even these don't give the full sense of what he achieved or why he acted in a certain way at a particular time.

In this case it took a long time for a significant number of people to gather, some from further afield than others, some with different expectations than others – but they all had one thing in common, they all needed the bread of life.

We read later that the number of people was four thousand. Matthew in his record specifically states that this number was *besides* woman and children. He mentions this on both the occasion of feeding the five thousand *and* the four thousand here. So the mass of people is significantly more than the simple number given. We'll have a closer look at this later.

The first time Christ performed this feeding miracle was on the opposite side of the Sea of Galilee and although there is no direct reason given as to why these two incidents should be compared, a comparison is important to the record. This is even evident in Jesus' opening words to his disciples.

In the first instance on the western side of Galilee, they were in a predominantly Jewish area. Here on the eastern side of Galilee they were in a predominantly Gentile population. At the feeding of the 5000 in the Galilean area, *his disciples came to him. "This is a remote place," they said, "and it's already very late. Send the people away so that they can go to the surrounding countryside and villages and buy themselves something to eat."*

Here in Decapolis Jesus needed to raise the issue. It was less than a day since the disciples were previously concerned but on this occasion it had already been three days!

Why such a difference? Have the disciples been negligent? Have they sat around for three days and failed to recall the feeding of the 5,000? Were they not hungry themselves?

Although Mark is not specific, it is not difficult to imagine that there was a certain tone in Jesus' voice towards his disciples as he is obviously challenging them. First to have faith and secondly to draw from them a reason as to why it had fallen to him to raise the issue of hungry masses.

Just reading the incident as it is can lead us to think, 'Why didn't the disciples put two and two together here?' Without a doubt they hadn't entirely blanked the feeding of the five thousand from their minds, surely not all twelve of them! Why was it that they found themselves on the end of such a question from Jesus?

There are a couple of possibilities why this is so, indeed it may be that it was a combination of factors. They may have been so hungry themselves that they were not 'thinking straight' but they did have *some* food. The absence of much civilisation around them may have led them to conclude that this wasn't going to be a good time to go shopping for lunch, so perhaps they had put the possibility on hold until they were nearer a food market.

But perhaps the best indication is the words that *both* Matthew and Mark use to describe the scene. They are both consistent in this and when we understand the nuances of the words they use it's a remarkable window on the situation.

At the feeding of the five thousand we read in both records that the KJV uses the term, they were in a *desert place*. Now, the disciples didn't know a desert as we do. To us a desert is something like the Simpson, Sahara or Sonoran – desolate, seemingly lifeless places with no rainfall, only a few blades of grass and a couple of tumbleweeds. Not so in the time of Jesus for that area was (and is again today!) a fertile and abundant area. And the record bears this out because Jesus also instructed the disciples to seat the people down *on the grass*.

The words 'desert place' mean an empty or *solitary place*, hence the NIV translation as *'a remote place'*. Not that it was dry and dusty, just that it wasn't used, cultivated or inhabited. In fact the disciples urged Jesus to send the people into nearby villages to buy food.

However, when we come to the feeding of the four thousand both Gospels change and call it a *wilderness place* (KJV). In their language this change in words was only a tiny difference – but it creates an entirely different picture. They call the wilderness a *place of solitude* (instead of a *solitary place*).

While we don't depend on knowing the difference in these two expressions to explain the place in which the disciples find themselves, it does help to explain *their thinking* on the occasion. Although it doesn't describe the scene exactly, I'll use the following descriptions to bring it into a modern idiom which gives a better sense of the difference. At the feeding of the five thousand they found themselves in a *recreation reserve*; the place wasn't isolated from civilisation, just that it was a public space within easy walking distance of the shops. But the feeding of the four thousand happened in a space we would recognise more like a *national park*. Both are public spaces set aside for people to come and go and enjoy the outdoors – but we (as the disciples did) would think about food options more readily at a recreation reserve than if we were in a national park.

This is borne out in their reactions also; at the recreation reserve they were concerned with the cost of the provision, while at the national park they questioned where they'd even find enough food. So they were in a situation where they didn't expect a repeat of the miracle, it really just hasn't crossed their mind.

And it was in this setting that Christ encouraged them to push the boundaries of their faith. If we fed five thousand in a more amenable place, why can't we feed four thousand in this place?

Thus in considering the situation we recognise a real lesson for us and our own faith. If we can preach Christ at our community picnic – what's stopping us doing the same at a national holiday picnic? The message is the same: what he can do through us in one place he has shown himself more than ready to do in another!

And so it extends to other facets of our faith and works. It's not just what we do, nor how we react or expect something to be - it's about how we *think* – '*...with God all things are possible.*'

Jesus was hoping that the disciples would ask for the repetition of the feeding of the 5000 but they didn't quite get it and so they asked, *"But where in this remote* [wilderness] *place can anyone get enough bread to feed them?"*

So far were their thoughts from feeding so many, that they unwittingly said 'feed', and they used a word meaning to feed as one fed livestock with an abundance of grass. They seemed to have forgotten that at the feeding of the five thousand there was not only so much food left over but the people themselves were sitting on the *grass*. This may not have been as luxurious in a national park – but I doubt Jesus would have missed their ironic choice of words.

It's not entirely unusual for that time though to think in different terms. Bread didn't come in packets but came from small-scale bakers, so perhaps the disciples were thinking of the process rather than just a finished loaf or two. And they were not entirely without care, for they had provided something for themselves and Jesus to sustain them during their travels.

"How many loaves do you have?" Jesus asked. "Seven," they replied.

Again we have some insight into the situation. At the feeding of the 5,000 Jesus asked them, *"How many loaves do you have?"... "Go and see." When they found out, they said, "Five--and two fish."* He dispensed with the call for them to *'go and see'* in this miracle with the 4,000, because there was even less expectation of finding food in this wilderness place. And the crowds would have already consumed most of whatever food they had brought with them. Which in part is why Jesus waited three days to perform the miracle – to exhaust the opportunity to explain the miracle by any another means other than the power of God through his actions.

But he was also testing their memory. Had they really forgotten the feeding of the 5,000? They said, *"But where in this remote place can anyone get enough bread"* – Jesus had started with bread and fish before and the miracle was simple multiplication. But Jesus could turn the very stones they were sitting on into bread if he wanted to.

And this time he was asking them to *give their own food*. I think there is a lesson in that. We can *take* from the Word so much but there will be times when we are required to *give* of ourselves instead. It's one thing to be able to just turn up at a function but it's quite another to be able to host it and take pride in being able to serve others as our Lord Jesus did.

The real miracle was in changing minds. All the disciples saw were seven measly loaves – while Jesus was looking at the potential of changing 4,000 or more *minds*!

Last year I moved into new offices where there are many other businesses and people around me. At home one night I cooked more meat for my meal than I needed; no problem, I could take it to work for lunch the following day. On the way to work I stopped to buy a bread roll to put this surplus meat in. There were people in front of me buying bags of bread to feed their families, I felt a bit silly asking for one bread roll - so I asked for two.

Now you may think two's not a big difference to one – but that day it was. When it came to lunchtime I found I *still* had more meat than would fit in one roll, I don't think it had multiplied but there was certainly more than I thought I had prepared. What to do? There was no way I was taking it home again for a third meal of the same thing! So I asked the lady in the office next door, "I've more than I can eat for lunch, would you like me to make you lunch today?" After all, two bread rolls is definitely a lot more than one now.

She enjoyed it immensely and I soon found out she'd told others! 'Where's our lunch?' they came around and joked. Being of a disposition that jumps first and thinks later, I said, 'Come down on Friday and I'll give you lunch'. Six people did – and that's how 'Foody Friday' started.

Some Fridays I lose count of how many turn up, but there's always enough to go around. 'What's on for Foody Friday, JB?' everyone asks on Monday, they look forward to it and offer to bring something – some Fridays I have to take home more than I bring! There's an outpouring of abundance.

Where there was once a melange of disparate business and people now there is a community. People mingle, talk, share and stop to think about other people. They offer to do my lawns if I'm away, look after my dog, they bring food from their gardens, answer my phone – one lady sent her husband over to my house last weekend to help fix the fence!

They know I'm interested in religion and history. They stand around eating on Fridays and ask questions like, 'What do you think about Christmas?' or 'How come Jews don't eat pork' and 'Is there really a trinity?'

Minds have changed. They think, care, offer, share, enquire, aspire, seek and desire more than mere work-a-day existence now.

I don't think it's exclusively food that does this. But it's interesting to consider how many times Jesus used food, either literally or in parable to convey his message and transform minds in the most wonderful way.

At the feeding of 5000 they found five loaves and two fish. Here at the feeding of 4000 they had seven loaves and a few fish. Five, of course, is speaking of grace in feeding of the 5000 but when we come to the 4000 we see there are seven loaves and this represents *spiritual completeness*.

The difference is that where grace was provided by Christ in the feeding of the 5000, whilst he is also present in the feeding of the 4000 more is required - and that *more* is required from the disciples themselves. The principle we see in this is that spiritual completeness needs input from us.

God created a world predestined in His foreknowledge of what was going to happen ahead - but it still requires a commitment from those hearers of the Word to be doers of the Word before God will be reflected *all in all,* because that is what spiritual completeness is.

Paul takes this point up in Colossians. There are deeper concepts that we need to understand which Paul elaborates on as he talks about this spiritual completeness. I'll quote from the KJV because it makes the words clearer in this instance: Paul puts it this way, *For in him* [Jesus] *dwelleth, all the <u>fullness</u> of the Godhead bodily. And ye are <u>complete</u> in him, which is the head of all principality and power.*

Notice these two words, the word 'fullness' and the word 'complete'. The word fullness does not quite translate into English like it does in the original and we don't have to go into itty bitty words all the time to get the meaning. We get the basic meaning by reading it as it is here, but if we look further at *fullness* and *completeness* we realise a wonderful principle.

Fullness is the word *pleroma* which means to be fully filled like a victualled ship. A modern example is that you fill up your motor car with fuel before you go for a long drive because if you do not have a full tank of fuel you will not arrive. It is the same as the term we often use today in to 'fill up before you go'. As they would victual a ship they would fill it up with all the ropes, food, fresh water and all the masts, sails and the pickled onion barrels, the bread, the wine – then the ship was 'full' and ready to go. This is what this word means in Colossians. In Christ dwells all the *filled-up-ness, ready-to-go-ness* of God.

And ye are complete in him, which is the head of all principality and power. Although the word *complete* is different, the Apostle is actually making a play on words because where the first word was *pleroma* this word is *plerou* which means 'filled to the brim'. He is using two well-known trading terms. Paul puts the two together here and says Jesus is filled like a victualled ship and we are filled to the brim. He is the ship God provided filled with all the barrels, and we are all the barrels on board, full to the brim. So Christ is filled-up, we are full to the brim and we're ready to set sail.

What's interesting about this is that Paul is saying, 'You <u>are ready</u> to go now'. Spiritual completeness is measured differently to worldly or material completeness.

It's really important to understand this. I'm guilty and I know other people are too, of saying, "When I know more I'll preach Christ and life everlasting". Or, "I'll just get the kids through college and then I'll dedicate myself to mission work - after all that's what I want to do with my *life*."

Jesus sent doubters, rebels, misfits, amateurs, uneducated, poor, homeless and otherwise totally unsuitable disciples to give a message to the whole world which was the most important message ever given – a matter of life and death!

Spiritual capacity is not how much spiritual readiness you can hold – it's how much capacity you have to dare let go. That's what Christ did – this is what *transforms*. Isaiah prophesied, *Therefore will I divide him a portion with the great, and he shall divide the spoil with the strong; because he hath **poured out** his soul unto death: and he was numbered with the transgressors; and he bare the sin of many, and made intercession for the transgressors.*

Grasping for something, which is the opposite to letting go, was what got us into trouble from the beginning! ... *When the* *woman saw that the fruit of the tree was good for food and pleasing to the eye, and also <u>desirable for gaining wisdom, she took some</u> and ate it. She also gave some to her husband, who was with her, and he ate it.* Christ was all about undoing this process.

Spiritual completeness is accepting that we don't know it all, going (obeying) and *letting* the process transform us and others. Desiring to gain wisdom certainly led Eve to transform Adam – she poisoned him!

I'm taking this to the extreme, true as it may be, to make a point. It's spiritual poison to get stuck in a mindset that says, 'I can't let my light shine because I don't know how much oil I'll need'. This thinking is stultifying, transfixing, incapacitating, debilitating.

Spiritual completeness is the opposite. It's the mind that embraces personal change; that trusts even to the point of giving your life. Can I do that? Honestly? No, certainly not yet anyway – I'll keep trying though. However I do know someone who has...

He told the crowd to sit down on the ground. When he had taken the seven loaves and given thanks, he broke them and gave them to his disciples to distribute to the people, and they did so. They had a few small fish as well; he gave thanks for them also and told the disciples to distribute them.

The record is not obvious but it does read as though they set the bread before people and *then* found a few small fishes afterwards which they gave out to eat as well.

It may have been a Foody Friday moment; someone thought they'd give something too. Matthew's record makes it sound like the disciples had the fish or at least found them pretty quickly after breaking the bread.

If we look at these records carefully we notice one tiny little difference in Christ's actions. In the account of the feeding of the 5000 he *looked to Heaven* and gave thanks but when feeding the 4000 we discover that he simply gave thanks. Matthew and Mark who record the instances both give exactly the same account for both miracles; he looked to heaven and gave thanks when among the Jews but among the Gentiles he just gave thanks.

There's some speculation as to why this was so, I think the only clue, if you can call it that, is that is Matthew says prior to this miracle that *they glorified the God of Israel*. Being Gentiles they may not have known exactly who the God of Israel was and therefore 'where' He was. They knew where their gods were – all over the place!

So the simple action of looking to heaven before giving thanks may well have confused the multitude, especially some thousands or so who were out of earshot. There may have been speculation later or 'Chinese whispers' as to what Jesus said, but at least no one would argue about *which* god he acknowledged as he didn't look in any specific direction!

We noted in the feeding of the 5,000 that the people were instructed to sit down in ranks on the green grass, but at the feeding of the 4,000 to just sit down on the ground where they were. In Galilee there had been green grass but in this wilderness place however, the ground-covering was less salubrious. Jesus *organised* the Jewish miracle. People were organised to sit in little groups and that suits the Hebrew or Jewish character, to sit and be organized like that. In the Gentile situation it seemed to be enough to say, "Ok, everybody, calm down, sit down and be quiet for a minute."

Since they were in a Gentile area (the Decapolis), there were probably language difficulties in trying to organise every one into companies of 100 or 50 as on the first occasion. So, in a way it was a precursor of how the Gospel of the Bread of Life was to go forward to the Gentiles. Some things would have to be done differently and this incident would not be lost on the Apostles and disciples in later years.

It's also worth noting the practicalities of having the people sit. There was order. It doesn't take a lot of imagination to guess how more than 4000 hungry people could cause quite a stampede! So there was control, everyone got their amount and hence there was little opportunity for people to come around again and again while others went without. The simple action of sitting kept everyone orderly.

While there was more than enough food to go around, in fact so much that they couldn't eat it all, Jesus wasn't going to give occasion for the miracle to turn sour for anyone. And although it is a seemingly small thing to record, it demonstrates both his ability as an administrator and as one with sensitivities to the nature of people.

It was *Jesus* who took the seven loaves and *gave them to his disciples to distribute*. Earlier he'd said to the Syrophoenician woman 'it is not meet to take the children's bread, and to *cast it unto the dogs*'. What is the difference here? I believe it is plainly a message to the disciples that the case of the Syrophoenician woman was one of him dealing with *her* faith but this interaction between Christ and the disciples is not a message on individual faith but a lesson to the disciples *to serve*.

Personal faith is good for growth. Miracles and healing are enlightening. But to feed and to look after many was something more important that Jesus was teaching the disciples. Although it was Christ who performed the miracle the disciples were sent to distribute the food.

The people ate and were satisfied. Afterward the disciples picked up seven basketfuls of broken pieces that were left over. What are we meant to see in these broken pieces? Obviously the fragments of bread, the filling of seven baskets were surplus to requirement. At the feeding of the 5,000 twelve baskets were taken up. We have already seen seven as the number of spiritual completeness, whereas the twelve baskets taken up is referring to the provisions for Israel.

Seven baskets being taken up is again spiritual completeness in Christ. So not only is the ship fully victualled and full – they are overflowing! It is this completeness that therefore embraces the Gentile in God's scheme – in fact it cannot be complete without them when it is His purpose to fill the earth, *all of it*, with His glory through this abundant grace as found in His Son.

John writes of this fullness, this complete transition to hope as, *'of his fullness have all we received, and grace for grace. For the law was given by Moses, but grace and truth came by Jesus Christ'.*

Consider that little phrase *'grace for grace'*. Have you ever questioned what this means? There's actually a clue in there because John goes on to say, *'for the law was given by Moses'*. What does that mean? Let's think about this 'grace for grace.' Where in the Law of Moses do you have a similar phrase? It doesn't have the word grace in it. Grace is predominantly a New Testament word.

In fact the term as grace found in the Old Testament invariably means finding acceptance between two people, such as 'if I have found grace (favour) in thy sight'. It's not until one or two instances of it in the Psalms – well beyond the Law of Moses - that the term means anything like what we know grace to be. Grace in the Old Testament is far more akin to what we would call mercy.

And of his fullness have all we received, and grace for grace. For the law was given by Moses – there is a comparison being drawn in these words! In the Law it was an eye for an eye, a tooth for a tooth, a hand for a hand, a foot for a foot and a breach for a breach. Do you see what the Apostle John is illustrating for us here? It is an interesting term, isn't it? Grace for grace. It does not have a connotation of tit for tat, or this for that. It's giving, not taking.

I've used the King James translation in this instance because other versions have missed the point about the Law of Moses and tried to modernise the verse without picking up the way John is making a comparison between the Old Law and the New Covenant.

So it is a beautiful illustration of *representative reflection*. It is like a mark pressed into the clay by a seal and line for line it is in there - replicated, image for image, like for likeness - it is exactly the same. And therefore grace for grace.

I'm going to digress here very briefly with an example because I want to define 'grace' – at least as it is used in the New Testament, because it's a popular theme among some Christian groups and many of them are wildly off the mark when it comes to understanding grace. This example has elements that run deeper throughout the Scripture and you'll guess some of them, but at its heart grace is a beautifully simple concept:

In my back yard is a lovely apricot tree. If you jumped my fence and helped yourself to my apricots I'd rightly be a little annoyed that you've denied me a prized jar or two of my favourite jam. But not being overly precious, I forgive you and kindly raise the issue with you and suggest that you ask next time. In this instance I have shown *mercy* by not enforcing my right to eat my own fruit.

However, if I go out of my way to speak with you and say, 'Listen, I have some apricots on my tree, I'd really be happy to share them with you. I'll leave the back gate open – you're welcome to come in and help yourself any time you like.' Then that's *grace*!

Grace for grace is not taking *from* as in eye for an eye. Grace for grace is taking *on*. It is taking on that *likeness*. Paul loves this concept and he goes after it enthusiastically and I think he explains it magnificently.

And we know that in all things God works for the good of those who love him, who have been called according to his purpose. For those God foreknew he also predestined to be conformed to the image of his Son, that he might be the firstborn among many brothers and sisters. And those he predestined, he also called; those he called, he also justified; those he justified, he also glorified.

Wonderful concept! Just the way Paul lets it flow here, we can read it so quickly and logically as he charges into it. Those He predestined, He called. Those He called, He justified. Those He justified, He also glorified. Simple, it's giving on top of giving.

There is a symbol of this abundance in the miracle of feeding so many people. So great was the provision that there was plenty left over. The words 'broken pieces' means fragmented bread. Why was it all broken? Because Jesus broke it when he distributed the food. It wasn't that everyone only ate half a loaf and left their crusts. This was bread that hadn't been touched, it wasn't food scraps. It was as if the bread was multiplied or replicated the same as the piece before it. Line for line, grace for grace.

Not wanting to waste the food they collected seven baskets full of this fragmented abundance. Remember our Syrophoenician woman? It was she who sought just a crumb that might fall from the table. What was first begged for in the start of this story of Jesus among the Gentiles, is now available in abundance. She was provided a spiritual crumb and her daughter lived, but now there is an abundance of physical bread that has sustained the people and helped them live, and still there was more.

What is a small morsel for one and what is a great abundance for another is the same thing. In the temporal world a little money is poverty and a lot of money is riches. However, in Christ a little is the same as a lot – because the abundance in him is spiritual and measured on another scale. Everything in Christ is equal, self-levelling. Paul makes this point to the Gentile Corinthians:

Our desire is not that others might be relieved while you are hard pressed, but that there might be equality. At the present time your plenty will supply what they need, so that in turn their plenty will supply what you need. The goal is equality, as it is written: "The one who gathered much did not have too much, and the one who gathered little did not have too little."

And that little bit on the end 'as it is written' is taken straight out of Exodus. Where? The gathering of Manna – of taking up the bread of Heaven! I'm not certain the Gentile Corinthians would have fully understood what Paul meant when he quoted this, unless there were Jews in the congregation with a spare, though rather expensive, handwritten copy of the first five books of the Hebrew Bible.

But *we* get it. It's spiritual in measure. The Bread of Life in his own abundance gives life.

In the feeding of the 5000 there were twelve baskets taken up and of the 4000, as we discovered, there were seven baskets taken up.

The baskets collected at the feeding of the 5000 were *kophinos*, like large lunch baskets they were a wicker basket similar to what you might take on a picnic. There were twelve of these which were probably large ones, like those bakers used in markets. We actually get our word coffin from this word kophinos because they were similar to what people were sometimes buried in. The word referred to what they were made of rather than their size. They were sturdy woven baskets that were fabricated to last some time.

But when we come to the feeding of the 4000, the type of basket changes from a kophinos to a *spyris*. A spyris was a large reed basket which is probably best described as a big trade basket. If you had harvested a lot of wheat you would put it in this kind of reed basket and then put it on a donkey or a cart to carry the cargo to a market or bazaar and sell your goods. They were made of reeds, so although they were sturdy they were for relatively short-term use compared with a kophinos.

There were seven baskets collected instead of twelve but the size of the basket was a lot bigger. This spyris basket is only mentioned in one other occasion in Scripture and that is when the disciples helped Paul escape by night and let him down over the wall of Damascus in a spyris.

Paul, a tent-maker who was used to sewing together sturdy structures made out of tough leather would have taken one look at the reed basket and known that it was a rather precarious vessel in which to be lowered over the side of a wall! He may have reflected later in his life on being saved by that spyris, and therefore able to deliver in great abundance the good news of Jesus to the Gentiles.

The number of those who ate was four thousand men, besides women and children. This is in keeping with the same record of feeding of the 5,000, there were 5,000 *beside women and children.*

For a bit of fun, here is a brace of mathematics for you - mathematics can be fun after all. Let's say there were as many women and children beside the men present – but that is just guessing because there were probably *more* women and children than men. But let's just conservatively say that there were an equal number of women and children as there were men, so this was not the feeding the 4,000 – it was the feeding of the 12,000!

We know they were hungry so let's assume they had two fish sandwiches each. In our terms a loaf is about 16 slices of bread so they would have needed 3,000 loaves of bread. At the average weight of a loaf the total is about 2.25 tons of bread.

They had a few small fishes. Let's say there were two sardines per sandwich; that is 48,000 sardines. By my reckoning that is about 8,000 tins of sardines. Can you imagine that! 8,000 tins of sardines, and the contents of a tin of sardines weighs around 100 grams, so that is about 800 kg of fish.

So in all, that is over 3,000 kilograms or three tons of food, whichever you prefer. If we squared this on a conventional pallet, topped it up with a little more because bread weighs less - we would have four and a half pallet loads of sandwiches just to feed these people. A loaf is about $4, a tin of sardines is about $1.15 - so to replicate this miracle the food bill would come in around $21,200!

We cannot really measure miracles. How do we measure the resurrection? It is impossible. How do we measure the value of someone having their sight restored? What is sight worth to you? We've done this simple exercise just to get us in the picture. Of course, there were seven great big trade baskets left over. I'll let you guess how much was in them altogether!

Here's a chart that shows some of the differences between the feeding of the 5,000 and the 4,000 if you want to consider them further:

Feeding of the 5,000	Feeding of the 4,000
Location was West of Lake Galilee.	Location was East of Lake Galilee.
Disciples were concerned that multitude had nothing to eat.	Christ was concerned that a multitude had nothing to eat.
Multitude went less than a day without food.	Multitude went three days without food.
Disciples concerned about the cost of the food.	Disciples concerned about where to buy the food.
The people sit in ranks.	The people just sit.
Sit on the green grass.	Sit on the ground.
Christ looks to Heaven and gives thanks.	Christ just gives thanks.
5,000 fed. (or approx. 15,000 estimating women and children)	4,000 fed. (or approx. 12,000 estimating women and children)
Five loaves.	Seven loaves.
Two fish.	A few small fishes.
Twelve medium baskets left over.	Seven large baskets left over.
Baskets were wicker *kophinos*.	Baskets were reed *spyris*.
Multitude want to make him King.	Multitude just content to hear his message.
Christ departs into a mountain to pray.	Christ takes a boat to the opposite coast.

After he had sent them away, he got into the boat with his disciples and went to the region of Dalmanutha. Matthew records that they came into the coasts of Magdala. There's not really any discrepancy between the two records as they are writing about *regions* and *coasts*, as a general area. Matthew who was with Jesus at the time seems to relate to the area, so he may have had family nearby. Magdala is generally accepted as Mary Magdalene's hometown (Mary of Magdala). Migdal, the modern name of Magdala is inland a kilometre or so, boats don't land at Magdala but they can land 'near' Magdala.

Dalmanutha, for those interested in words means a *slow firebrand*. It may have been some local reference Mark was alluding to, or a town he knew. Dalmanutha and Magdala are only mentioned once and in the same incident. Magdala means a *tower*. It may have been in antiquity that there was a tower there as part of some kind of forge or industry but academics have yet to find anything conclusive.

A LONELY LOAF

Now back in a predominately Jewish area of the Land, it was not long before the Pharisees found Jesus again. Perhaps they were missing him. They challenged him to 'show them a sign from heaven'. Surely they had seen or heard of the miracles he had done, nearby and abroad - how many signs did they need?

They didn't want just any sign or some miracle magic trick as they had convinced themselves these were. They wanted a sign from heaven itself – in other words they were demanding that he tell God what to do! 'You get God to tell us to believe in you and we'll think about it.'

It must have been so frustrating for Christ – he was after all fulfilling the Scriptures they claimed as 'theirs', the ones they deemed God-given. On top of that they'd already seen God's spirit in the form of a dove alight on him, and heard the voice from heaven proclaim, *"This is my Son, whom I love; with him I am well pleased."* They didn't want to credit this as a sign from heaven, and had conveniently forgotten about it.

And so he rightly tells them; *"When evening comes, you say, 'It will be fair weather, for the sky is red,' and in the morning, 'Today it will be stormy, for the sky is red and overcast.' You know how to interpret the appearance of the sky, but you cannot interpret the signs of the times. A wicked and adulterous generation looks for a sign, but none will be given it except the sign of Jonah."*

They could read great signs of weather but ignored what was happening around them. And why the sign of the prophet Jonah? Of course, Jesus would be in the earth three days before his resurrection but the key significance of Jonah's life was that through his message the Gentiles repented and turned to God!

The irony is that on the shores of Galilee (which means *a circuit*) Jesus had just completed an enormous circuit out to the Mediterranean, across the top of Israel, down through the midst of the Decapolis, back across the southern part of Lake Galilee – and here he was again having the same debate with the Pharisees. Talk about going in circles!

The Gentiles didn't need debate or demand some sign or require convincing that the New Covenant had arrived – they simply believed him. A great multitude would benefit from this circuit Jesus had taken, from the words and faith he instilled in the people but also in the preparation that he had given his disciples to be fishers of men – they were the next ripple in the great wave that has since covered the whole earth.

So Jesus and the disciples board a boat again and head 'home' to Bethsaida. And despite some lingering frustration with the

Pharisees, I don't think the meaning of that town's name would have been lost on our Lord – Bet-tzaida, *the house of fishing*.

The disciples had forgotten to bring bread, except for one loaf they had with them in the boat. However, Matthew makes it clear that they had already arrived when this was discovered, not as it sounds in Mark as if they were discussing it on the boat-ride home; *And when his disciples were come to the other side, they had forgotten to take bread.*(KJV)

Even if they were sailing at a sedate two knots the time to get from the coast near Magdala to Bethsaida was less than a couple of hours. They could not have been starving; surely they'd gone longer than that without something to eat before. So why did both Matthew and Mark recall this? Doesn't it make the disciples look 'needier' than is necessary?

Matthew and Mark are using it as a segue or pivot for Christ's words of wisdom that follow but it was also an important part of their duties that had entirely slipped their mind. The fact was that they had left the coasts of western Galilee, the breadbasket of the nation - and they were going *home*.

It was a temporary home for some of the disciples, as Jesus' ministry was based in the area but for others it was where they actually lived. Bethsaida was the hometown of James and John. Philip also was from Bethsaida, Peter and Andrew fished from Bethsaida and had a house in nearby Capernaum as well.

Wheat was grown in the west of Galilee; they would fish in Galilee and because they had boats they would trade with them as their boats were the natural means of transporting bread (the most important staple) to all their families.

We can assume that Peter's mother-in-law was still alive and probably his wife also. James and John's father Zebedee and their mother Salome were still at home. The disciples, the food providers were returning *home*, and it is quite an amusing little picture that the Gospel writers are illustrating for us!

Have you ever received a phone call that goes something like this; 'Can you pick up some bread and milk on your way home'? Sound familiar? How about a text along the same lines? Or *you* are the one primarily responsible for bread-fetching in your home – but you get home to find out you forgot it. And if you are married, or remember what happened when you were growing up and dad forgot to bring home something he well knew mum was expecting? Remember that? You can probably recall someone getting into a lot of trouble.

Imagine then, twelve disciples are about to walk in the door and it's probably going to go something like this:

'Where on earth have you been?!' *(Remember, mobile phone coverage hadn't got to Bethsaida, Sidon or the Decapolis yet!)*
'Well we were with Jesus. We walked all the way to Sidon,'
'SIDON?!'
'Yes, he healed a lady's daughter there. Then after that we went to the Decapolis.'
'THE DECAPOLIS?!'
'Yes, and Jesus healed a deaf and dumb man there. After that we headed south and he did this amazing miracle, you should have seen it – he fed 12,000 people bread and fish!'
'12,000?!'
'Then we went to where we usually get bread and had a bit of an argument with the Pharisees and guess what?'
'What?'
'I forgot to get bread...'
'YOU WHAT?!'

As usual, perhaps I'm hamming it up a little more than was the reality. But you get the point. Mark goes to the trouble of recording that they didn't have more than *one* loaf. Why write that? Because there were *Twelve* disciples, who for a short while at least were going to *separate* homes.

So although they'd probably enjoyed their adventure, they now remembered that there was a parallel reality. They may have been fledgling apostles but they were also husbands and sons with families and responsibilities. It's probably a bit cheeky to write this but I'll blame the Gospel writers for putting the picture in my head – I can imagine the twelve of them standing around on the dock, the magnitude of their forgetfulness dawning on them, one lonely loaf between the lot of them and Philip saying, 'Here Peter, you better have it. You've got a mother-in-law!'

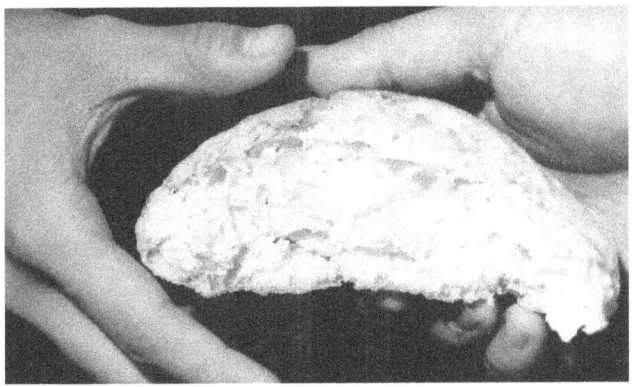

And it was into this predicament that Jesus injects a little heavenly wisdom: *"Be careful... Watch out for the yeast of the Pharisees and that of Herod."*

You can just imagine the disciples looking up from their dilemma totally agog. What did he just say? What has that got to do with anything?! What leaven? *They discussed this with one another and said, "It is because we have no bread."*

It wasn't that they didn't trust Jesus, nor that they didn't want to have faith. They were just in a different *headspace* as we would say today. They were caught between two worlds, one of spiritual thoughts and actions and another of the earthly and mundane.

Aware of their discussion, Jesus asked them: "Why are you talking about having no bread? Do you still not see or understand? Are your hearts hardened? Do you have eyes but fail to see, and ears but fail to hear? And don't you remember? When I broke the five loaves for the five thousand, how many basketfuls of pieces did you pick up?"
"Twelve," they replied.
"And when I broke the seven loaves for the four thousand, how many basketfuls of pieces did you pick up?"
They answered, "Seven."
He said to them, "Do you still not understand?"

Certainly, his message was that they shouldn't worry about not having enough bread. But there's more to it, hence his call to *beware of the leaven of the Pharisees*. Jesus was pointing out that they were duplicitous in their thinking. The disciples were *of two minds*.

Jesus described this leaven specifically in Luke's Gospel when he said, *"Be on your guard against the yeast of the Pharisees, which is hypocrisy."*

The disciples were not behaving like malicious or conniving hypocrites – but they *were* of two minds and Jesus was warning them that it was only a small step from one to the other – *beware*.

In the same chapter in Luke he goes on to say, *"Are not five sparrows sold for two pennies? Yet not one of them is forgotten by God. Indeed, the very hairs of your head are all numbered. Don't be afraid; you are worth more than many sparrows."*

The little Bible open on my desk at Luke has a heading at the top of the page which reads, 'The teaching about anxiety'. And I think that pretty much sums up where the disciples were.

Obviously someone with clinical anxiety is not going to be able to read this teaching about anxiety and be completely and immediately healed. But there are a lot of people who live in two minds, including those who have one headspace for Sundays and one for every other day of the week.

There are also simple people like me who the first time I come up against a challenge find myself scrambling to muster all the worldly wisdom I can find to beat it. Sometimes I'm the disciple who gets back in the boat and says, 'You guys go on ahead, I'll go back and get some bread for us,' instead of being the disciple that turns to my Lord and says, 'You've done it twice – I trust you'll do it again.'

Mark's record adds *and that of Herod*. What does this mean? There may be a couple of ideas but the one that seems to fit best this context is 'covetousness'. Herod among other dastardly acts had coveted and taken his brother's wife. We can probably take it to mean that just as two minds are in danger of falling into hypocrisy, so too anxiety over desires are but a short step away from covetousness – *beware*.

Matthew indicates that they seemed to get the message, *Then they understood that he was not telling them to guard against the yeast used in bread, but against the teaching of the Pharisees and Sadducees.*

We never find out what happens to the one lonely loaf. Perhaps that's deliberately left up to our imagination. What we are left with is a powerful message from the one and only, *Bread of Life.*

A BRAVE NEW WORLD

It is fascinating to imagine 'being on the road' with Jesus and what sights his disciples saw. The grandeur of changing landscapes, the broad expanse of the Mediterranean beckoning new lands beyond, the soaring heights of the mountains in the north, the vast spaces of the east.

The sights, sounds and colour of human life, the smell of the goat-herder they stopped to talk to, the rich effusion of spices traded in the markets and the colourful dress of people coming and going from many cultures.

It was all a foretaste, a glimpse of where the Gospel would go, of what lands it would travel to (and how!), what the people would hear, what new sons and daughters, these brothers and sisters would become as they coalesced into one loving, understanding and hope-bound community of believers.

It would be only a couple of years before the message first trickled over the borders of the Holy Land and then grew to a flood of religious transformation. Onwards and outwards it swept, ever seeking a void, ever desiring brave new worlds into which to pour its hope.

There were bumps on the road then as now. But the Truth in Jesus Christ has transcended its vulnerability to intervention – it has survived, it has maintained its credibility and above all its message of life-giving expectation.

I'm continually and pleasantly surprised *where* on this earth people are being called, sometimes in places I've never heard of let alone thought the Truth of the Gospel would penetrate. And it's also seen closer to home; in the addict who seeks salvation, the obsessive professional who seeks release and the person who thought he was a nobody and discovers he is someone indeed and has found value and worthiness in life.

What is it about the Gospel that makes it compelling and universal in its reach? As much as academic theologians may disagree – its success is really due to its simplicity. This simplicity together with its appeal to what is at the heart and interest of all humanity; life and the quality of it that makes the Gospel not only noteworthy but attractive – whoever you are.

The term Gospel is often described as 'Good News' or 'Glad Tidings'. And indeed it rather is! Our English word comes from the translation of the Latin term *bona adnuntiatio* (good announcement) into Old Saxon *godspell* which literally means 'good story'.

However, this belies the real core of what the Gospel is by way of its power to change lives. In the days of the Gospel writers they used the word *euangelion*, meaning 'reward for bringing good news'. But they would also have recognised this word as a contraction of the two words 'eu' (be well off) and 'angelos' (messenger) – or put together in *euangelion*, to be 'well off for a good message'.

It's not that the Gospel is just a good story – but that it makes us 'well off'. It's the only kind of 'well off' that transcends any other type. Today we most often use the term 'well off' in a financial sense. The further we go back in history the more it means 'favoured or rewarded'. That is why in its essence the Gospel cannot be compared with any other blessing. Nothing can offer what it does – eternal life.

Paul, as we saw earlier, said the Gospel was first preached to Abraham, *"Understand, then, that those who have faith are children of Abraham."*

And notice that he uses Abraham's *changed* name. He was born Abram which means 'exalted father' and became Abraham, 'father of a multitude'.

Abraham received many blessings; a son, vast herds and livestock, God even promised him a Land. But Paul singles out the greatest blessing; *Scripture foresaw that God would justify the Gentiles by faith, and announced the gospel in advance to Abraham: "**All nations** will be blessed through you."*

In the same chapter Paul ties this Gospel into the outworking of it in Christ; *The promises were spoken to Abraham and to his seed. Scripture does not say "and to seeds," meaning many people, but "and to your seed," meaning one person, who is Christ...*

*So in Christ Jesus **you are all children of God** through faith, for all of you who were baptized into Christ have clothed yourselves with Christ. There is neither Jew nor Gentile, neither slave nor free, nor is there male and female, for you are all one in Christ Jesus. If you belong to Christ, then you are Abraham's seed, and **heirs according to the promise**.*

It was always God's intention to redeem and reward the *whole* earth – reuniting everyone with Him in purpose and glory. This could not begin to happen until Jesus was among the Gentiles.

And now, thanks to God's gracious gift – he is.

www.ingramcontent.com/pod-product-compliance
Lightning Source LLC
Chambersburg PA
CBHW071303040426
42444CB00009B/1849